“To whom?
Who
art thou?”

“To thee would
I come,
into thy heart!”

PARSIFAL CONTAINER

Georg Baselitz
Alexander Kluge

Translated from the German
by Isabel Cole

Spector Books

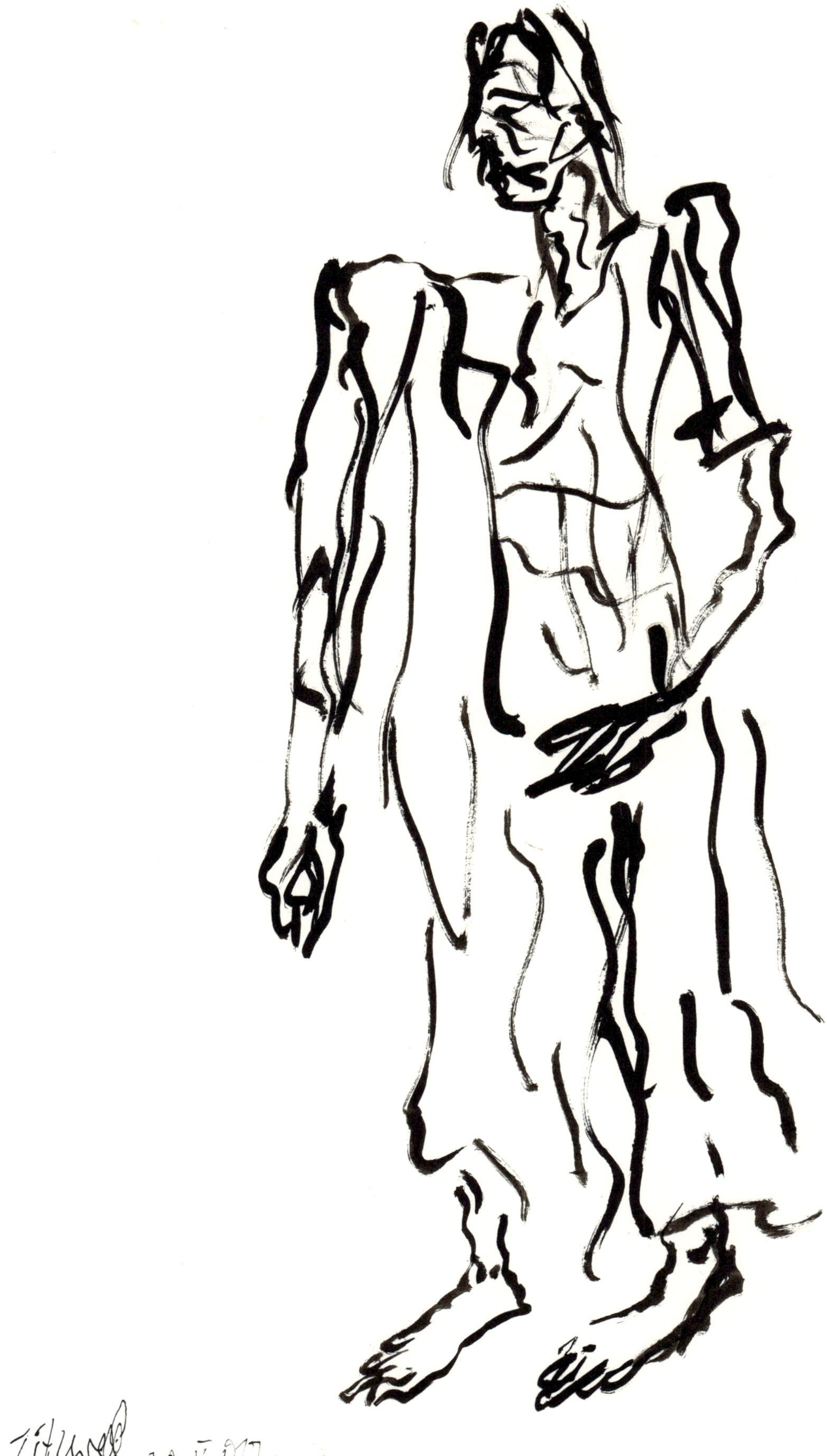

2017 Titurel

MOTIFS IN RICHARD WAGNER'S *PARSIFAL*

OVERTURE

Eucharist motif
Largo
Grail motif
Largo
Faith motif
Largo
Melancholy motif
Largo
Torment of sin motif
Rather stretched out

ACT ONE

Amfortas motif
Wildness motif
Kundry motif
Duty motif
Forest motif
Fool motif

Kundry's seduction motif
Wound motif
Spear motif
Good Friday motif
Swan motif
Herzeleide motif
Humility motif
Bell motif
Boys' chorus

ACT TWO

Grieving motif
Courtly love motif
Caressing motif
Flattering motif
Fighting motif
Flower girls
Yearning motif
Devotion motif

ACT THREE

Grail mourning motifs
Wandering motif
Atonement motif
Blossoming meadow motif
Mourning chorus
Miracle motif

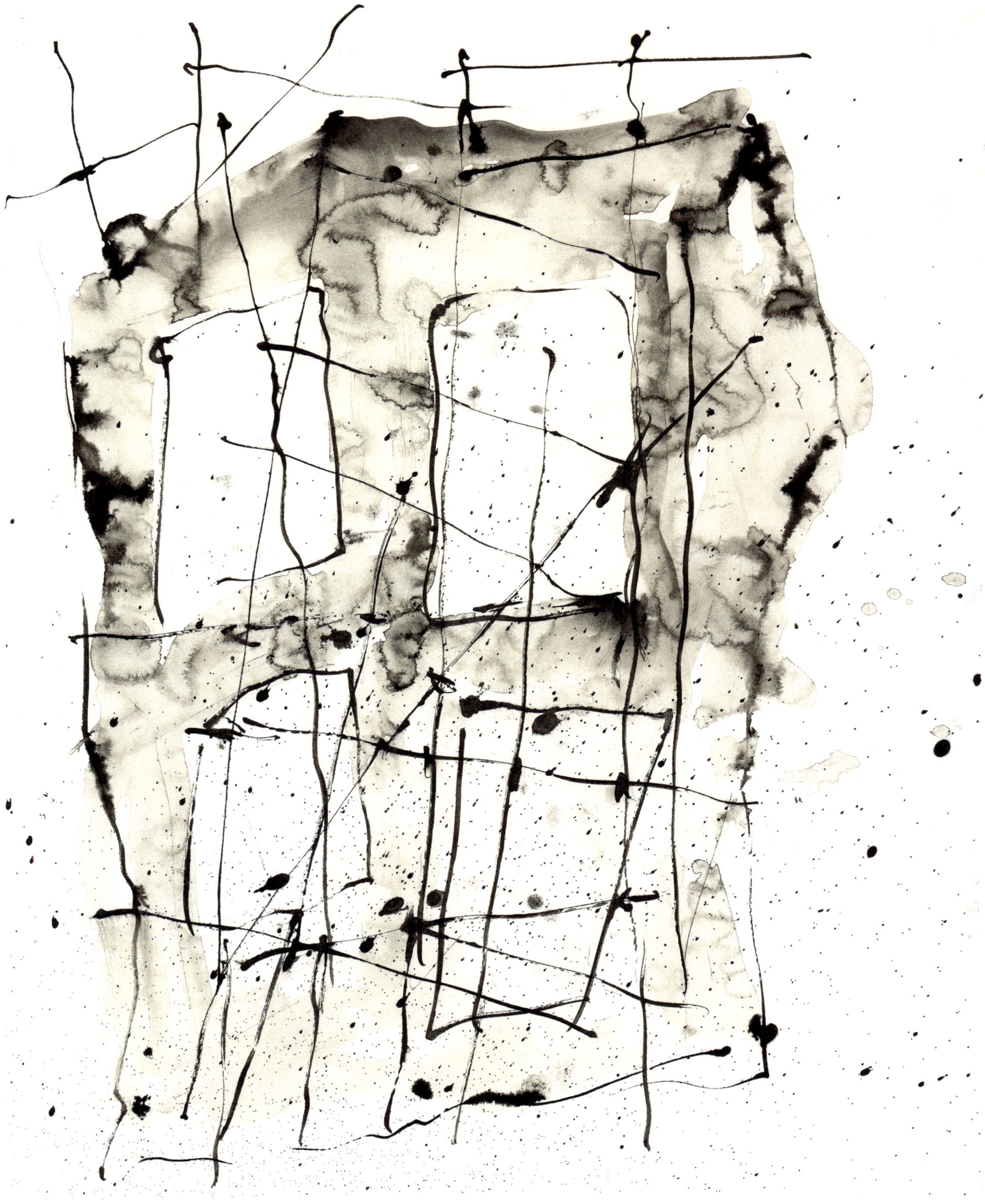

2017

Set design, rejected

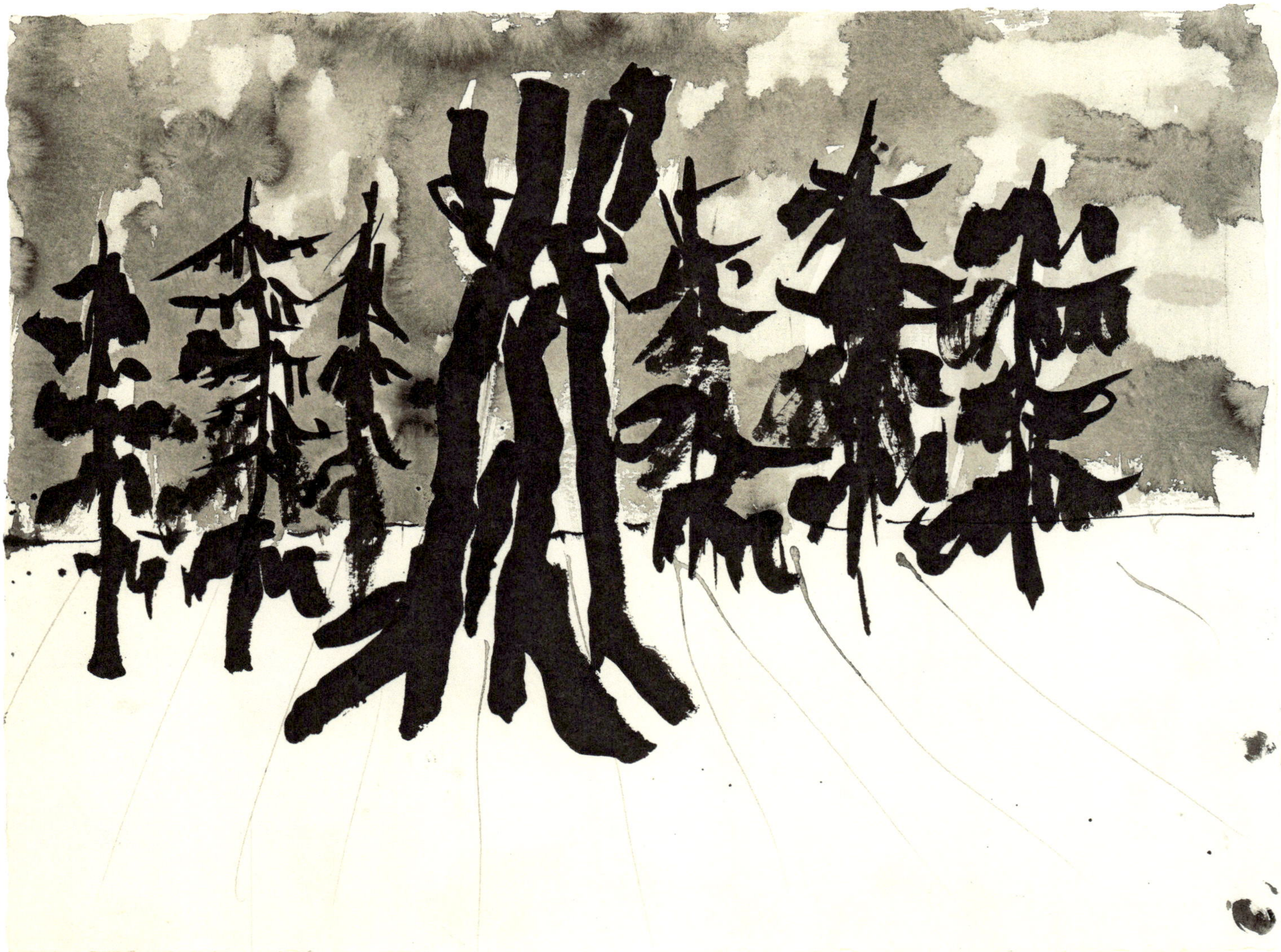

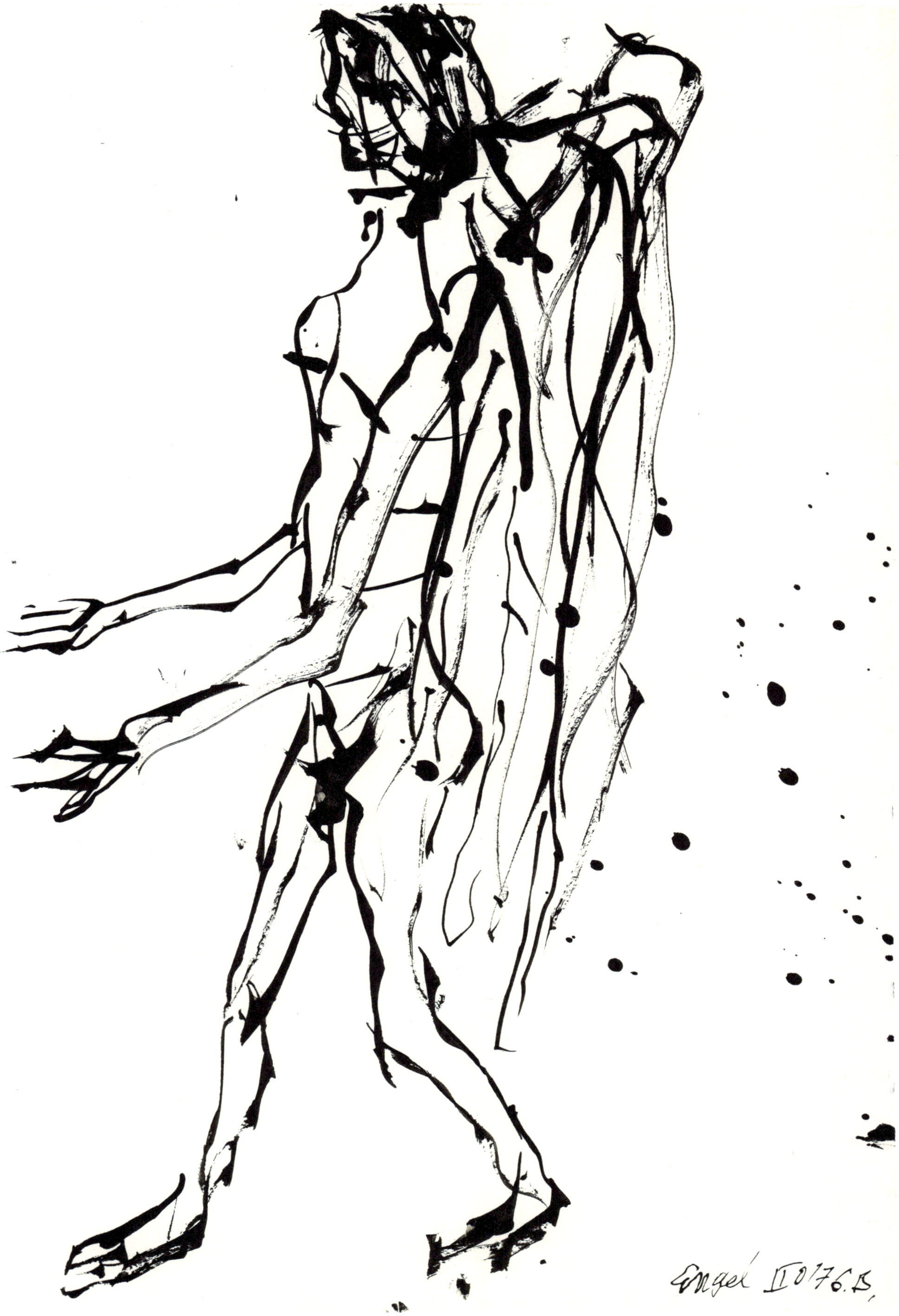

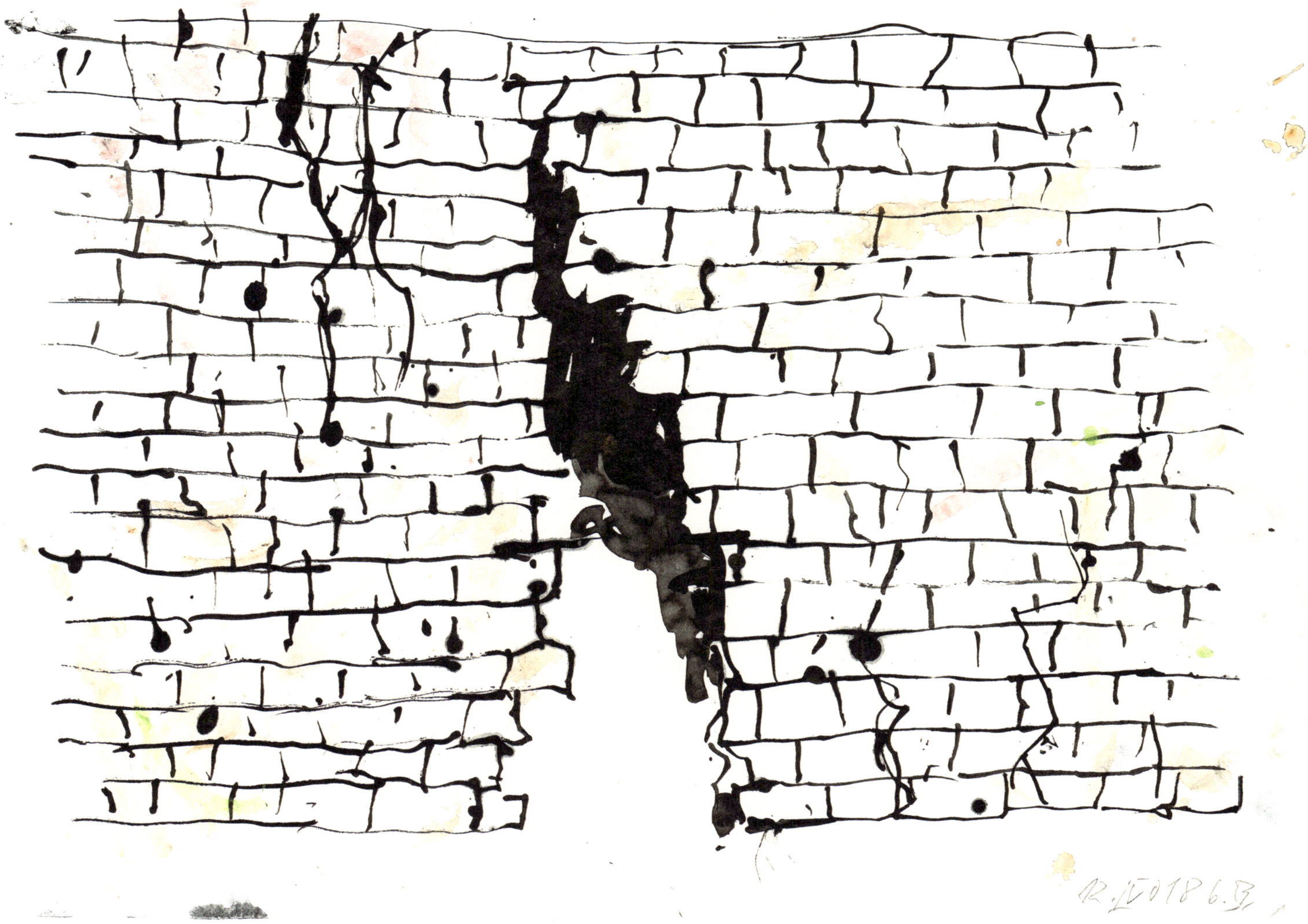

2018

Curtain

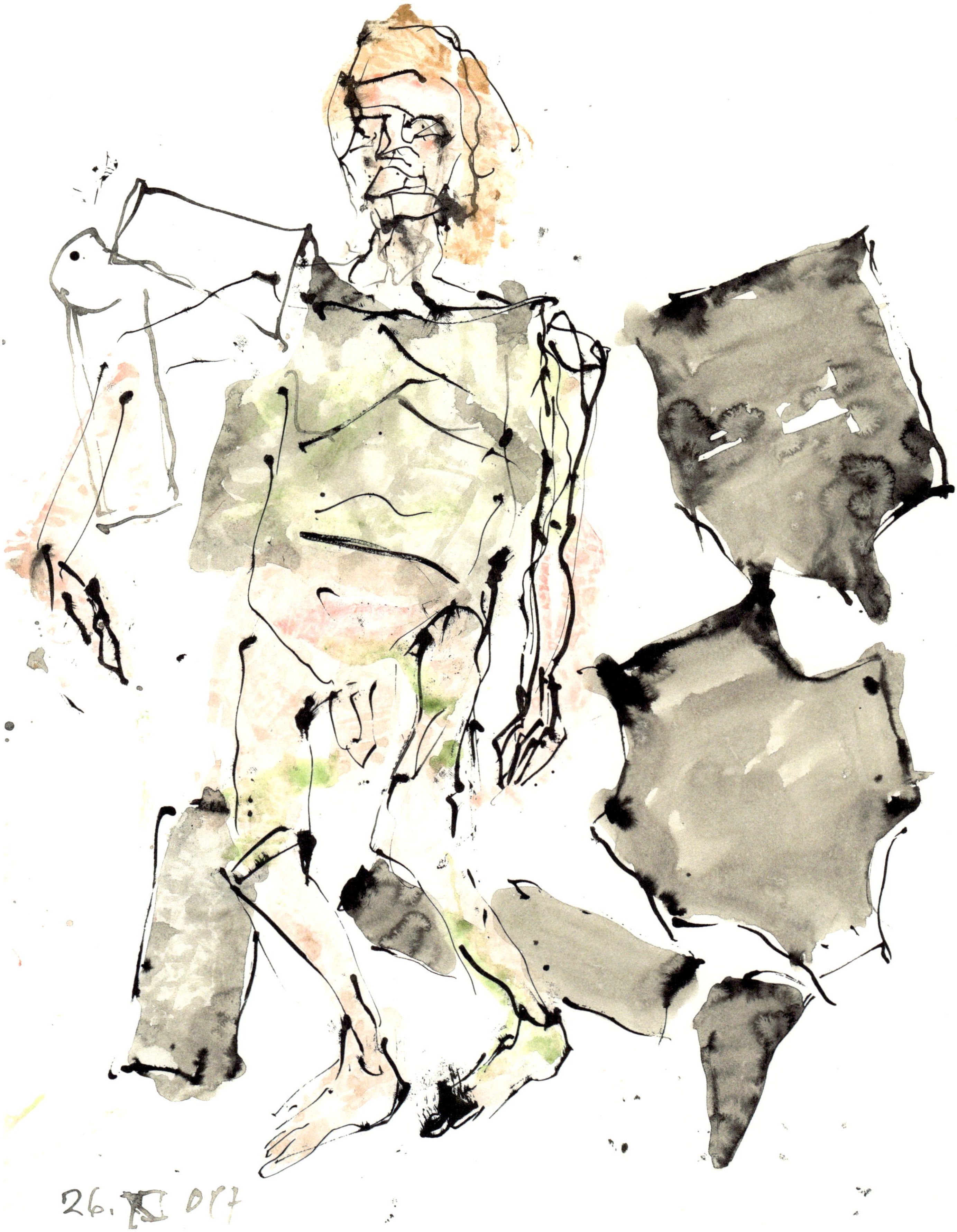

2017 Parsifal

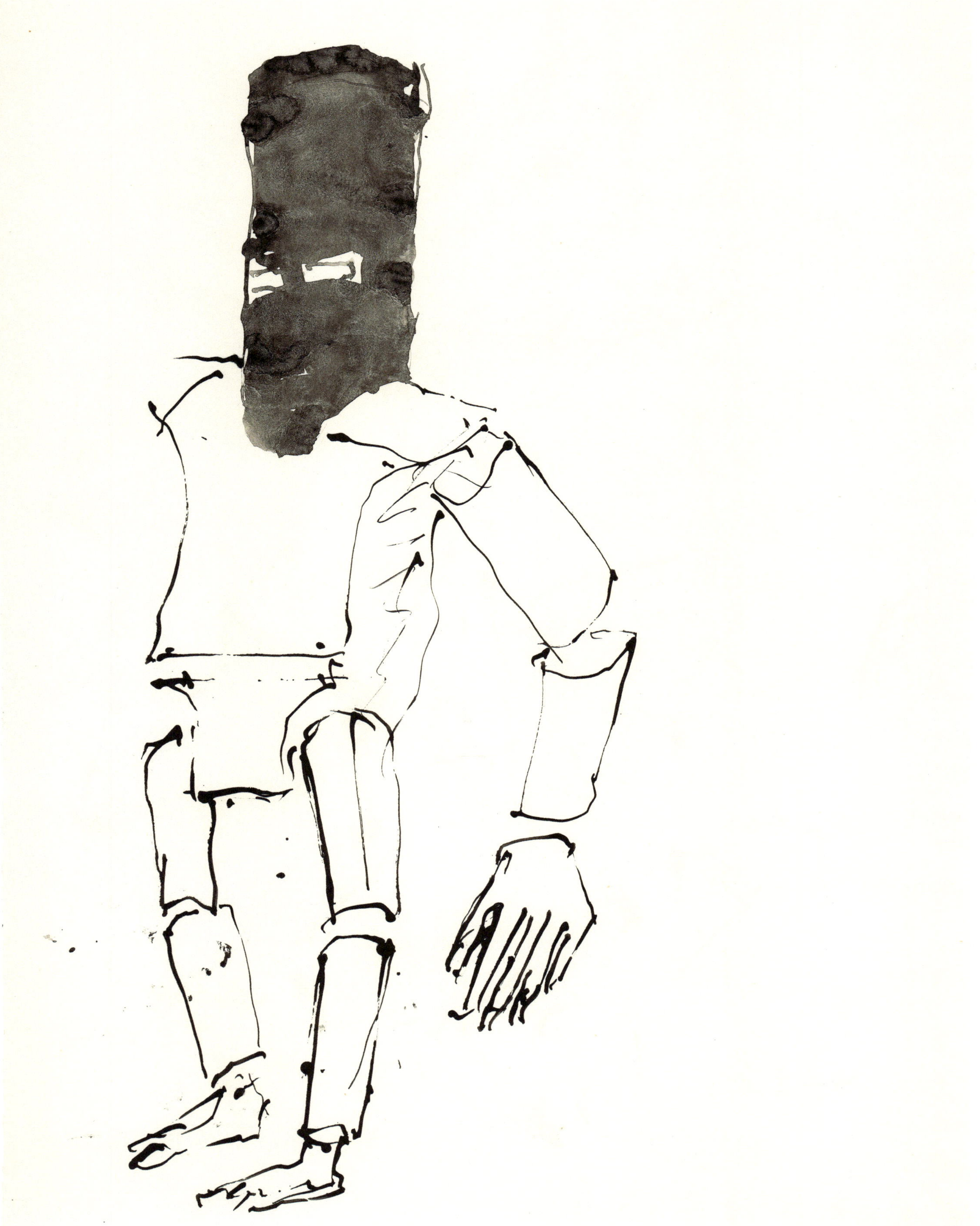

Parsifal 2017

WOULD A KNIGHT OF THE SORROWFUL COUNTENANCE (DON QUIJOTE) BE BETTER FOR EUROPE THAN A KNIGHT OF THE CHEERFUL COUNTENANCE (PARSIFAL)?

Shortly before turning 90, the writer Martin Walser spent two weeks flirting with the following question: Which literary devices would be required to turn the hero Parsifal into a German Don Quixote? He got the idea when, due to a misunderstanding, he'd ended up at a performance of Wagner's *Bühnenweihfestspiel* ("Stage-Consecrating Festival-Play"—the composer's term for his *Parsifal*). The opera was supposed to heighten the tourist appeal of a certain South German city's Easter-time music festival. With an effort, from out-of-character politeness, he sat through the four-hour performance. The singers were mediocre. But the "high-potential vacuum" represented for him by those four hours carved out of life's joys gave him the idea of going back to Wagner's source material. The verses he found there compensated for the Good Friday ordeal of the musical drama.

For which period of Central European history would a Don Quixote be desirable? In his outline, Walser sketched out a character in the spirit of Joseph von Eichendorff. This man takes a position with the EU administration in Brussels. In Athens he negotiates with representatives of the Greek finance ministry. He detects traces of ancient Greece in his negotiating partner. The bailout plan that he takes first to Brussels and immediately thereafter to Washington gets an incredulous reception at the session of the International Monetary Fund.

In those two weeks, Walser piled up pages and pages of notes. They told him what he wouldn't have known from simply thinking or feeling: that it seems a hero can't be invented by literary means (even Wagner failed at that). You have to go out in search of him. In the end, Walser had compiled 88 two-line verses excerpted from Wolfram von Eschenbach's works and Chrétien de Troyes' *Parsifal*. How fortunate it would have been for Central Europe had there been a "Central German Don Quixote" named Parsifal back during the Peasant Wars or World War II. ALWAYS THE WRONG HEROES!

THE NOBLE LAD BEGGED HER TO GIVE HIM A HORSE

There's a popular song from the 1940s about a little boy who wants a warhorse for Christmas ("Mamatschi, give me a horsey"). Later on, he's slaughtered in the war. On receiving the news of his death, his mother realizes that she shouldn't have put that toy horse under the Christmas tree. For a moment, the seasoned primary school teacher has a mind to overhaul child-rearing methods throughout Germany. Not because her child is dead, but because compulsory military service, that is, a piece of legislation, has long since deprived children and parents of the ability to decide whether to go to war. We'll need to dig deeper, she thought, in fact we need to abolish governments completely.

"OPE THE PORTAL!" "TO WHOM? WHO ART THOU?" "TO THEE WOULD I COME, INTO THY HEART!"

The name PARSIFAL means "straight through the middle." Also: "through the valley." Scene outside a castle gate: Enter a man in armor. "Open the portal!" The response: "To whom? Who are you?" The masked man replies:

> "I wish to come straight into thy heart, Madame!"

This line may have been corrupted by retranslations, but it does convey the directness of Parsifal's character.

"FROM THE SEA WILL I SUMMON THE GREATEST FORCE WHOSE SAILS JUNO'S BREATH E'ER FILLED"

At the war's very end, in April, 1945, the Panzergrenadier division "Parsifal" was formed from the remnants of twelve scattered Volksgrenadier divisions in TANNE IN THE HARZ MOUNTAINS. The equipment came from a depot near Goslar.

The outfit moved over the passes of the Harz, aiming to use forest paths in the Westerwald and the Siebengebirge to reach the south of France. There—according to the forestry office in Thale—a tunnel TWELVE METERS BENEATH A CASTLE RUIN hid a stone or vessel, soaked in blood. Mere molecules of the liquid it contained, or even the stone itself, could bring down Allied bomber squadrons. The outfit moved off in the rain.

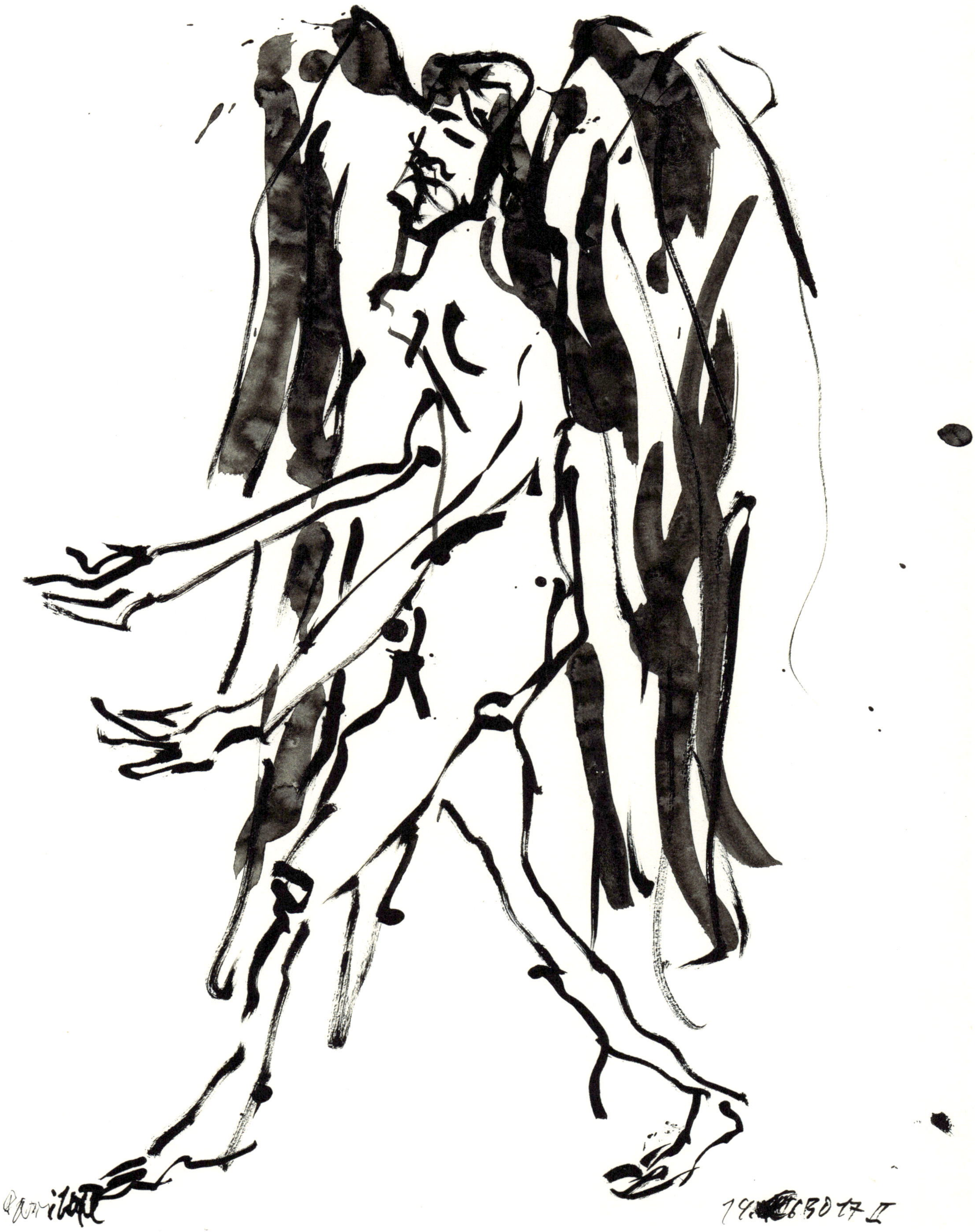

2017 Parsifal

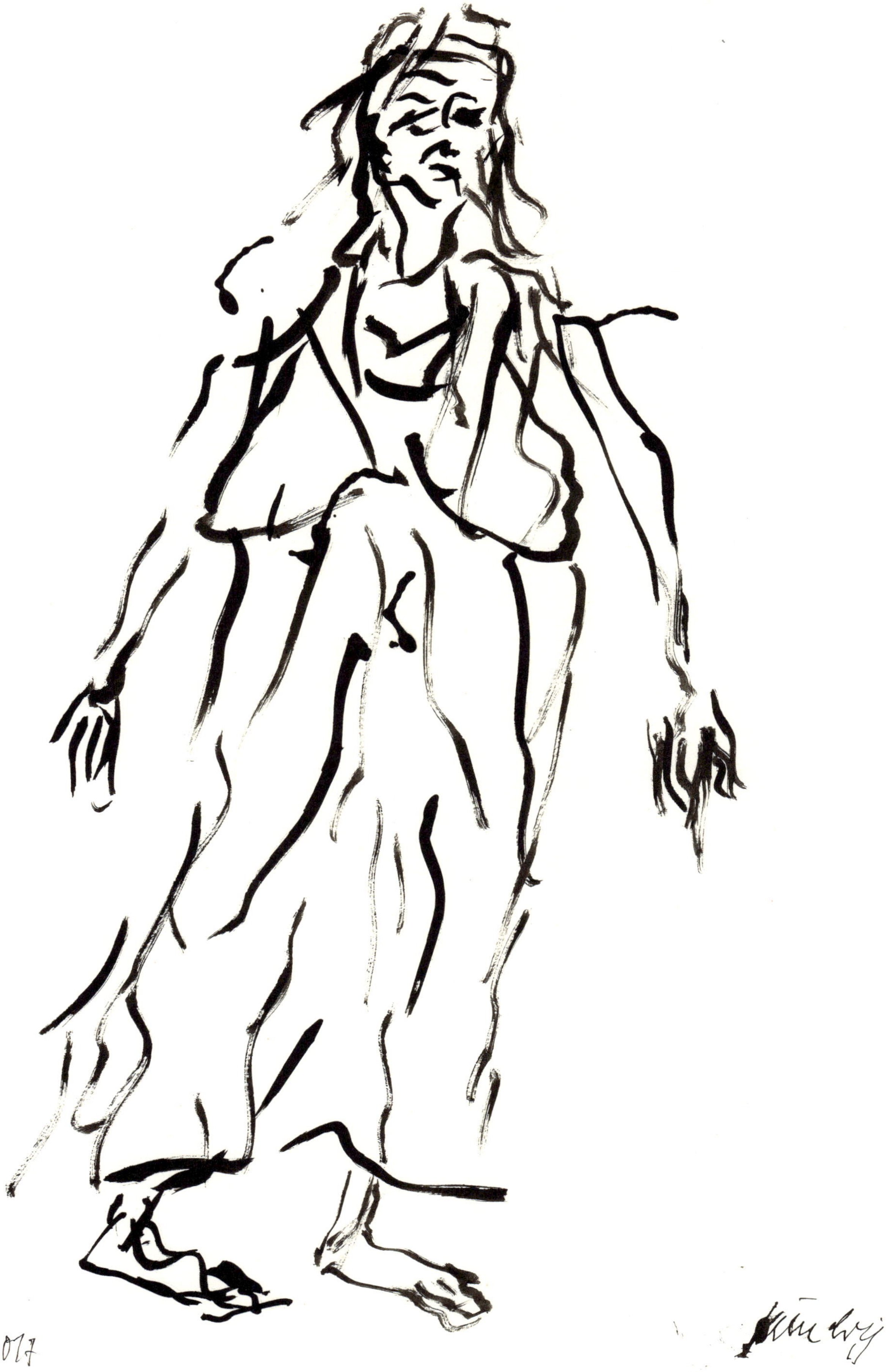

2017 Kundry

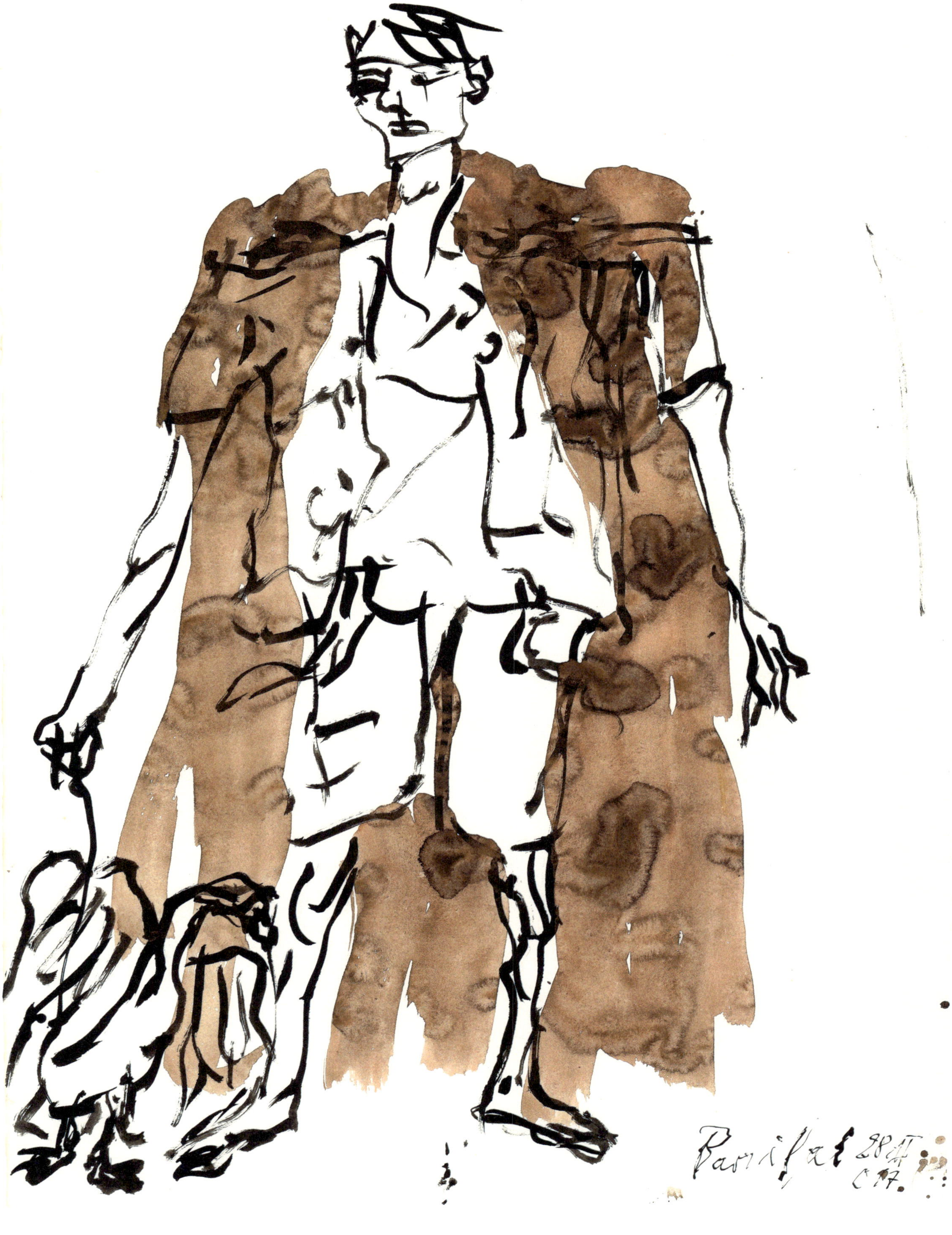

“The Lady Herzeloyde did not allow

INTELLIGENCE COMES FROM THE MOTHER'S SIDE

Queen Genevieve of Brabant, betrayed and cast out, retreats to a hut in the woods. A herd of deer gives her succor. She raises her child in seclusion. With Wotan's daughter Sieglinde it's another story. A refugee, hiding in the thickets, she does not survive the birth of her kid (a Gargantua) by even a minute. The naïve young hero shatters her pelvic bones. Or did it happen differently? Did the blacksmith Mime attempt to rescue the awkwardly oversized child with a cesarean section? But he hadn't mastered the ancient surgical technique, hadn't properly cleaned the knives and scissors he used. At any rate, the heroic youth grew up without a mother. He accepted no guidance from the sterling blacksmith with the less than sterling origins.

Things took quite a different course when the witty Herzeloyde—unable to persist in her privation and grief forever, feeling the tickle of laughter whenever she started weeping, a person heavy of spirit and light of heart (how does that translate into contrasting black/white or the greed of a magpie?)—actively equipped her beloved charge with an arsenal of fooleries. In a different society, all of them would have been rational. But such tutoring always contained a quantum of chicanery. Her nostrils still held the pungent scent of the hero's father Gahmuret.

RAISED WITH MOTHER WIT

On learning of the death of her husband Gahmuret, who had left without even waiting for his son Parsifal to be born, and then died in the Caliph's service in the distant Southeast, Herzeloyde withdrew to a cave in the forest of Soltane. She had but one aim: to protect her son Parsifal. She wanted to give him an alternative upbringing, prepare him for a different life. He was a tiny boy. Teachable as a dog.

Each of her topsy-turvy pieces of advice—each of her errors, measured by the status of a courtly knight—was an arrow to the heart of the "realities." Those realities, like living beings, later responded with arrows of their own, striking the rather deranged-acting Parsifal. Even by the time an older knight had taken him under his wing, HE WAS STILL WEARING FOOL'S MOTLEY UNDER HIS ARMOR.

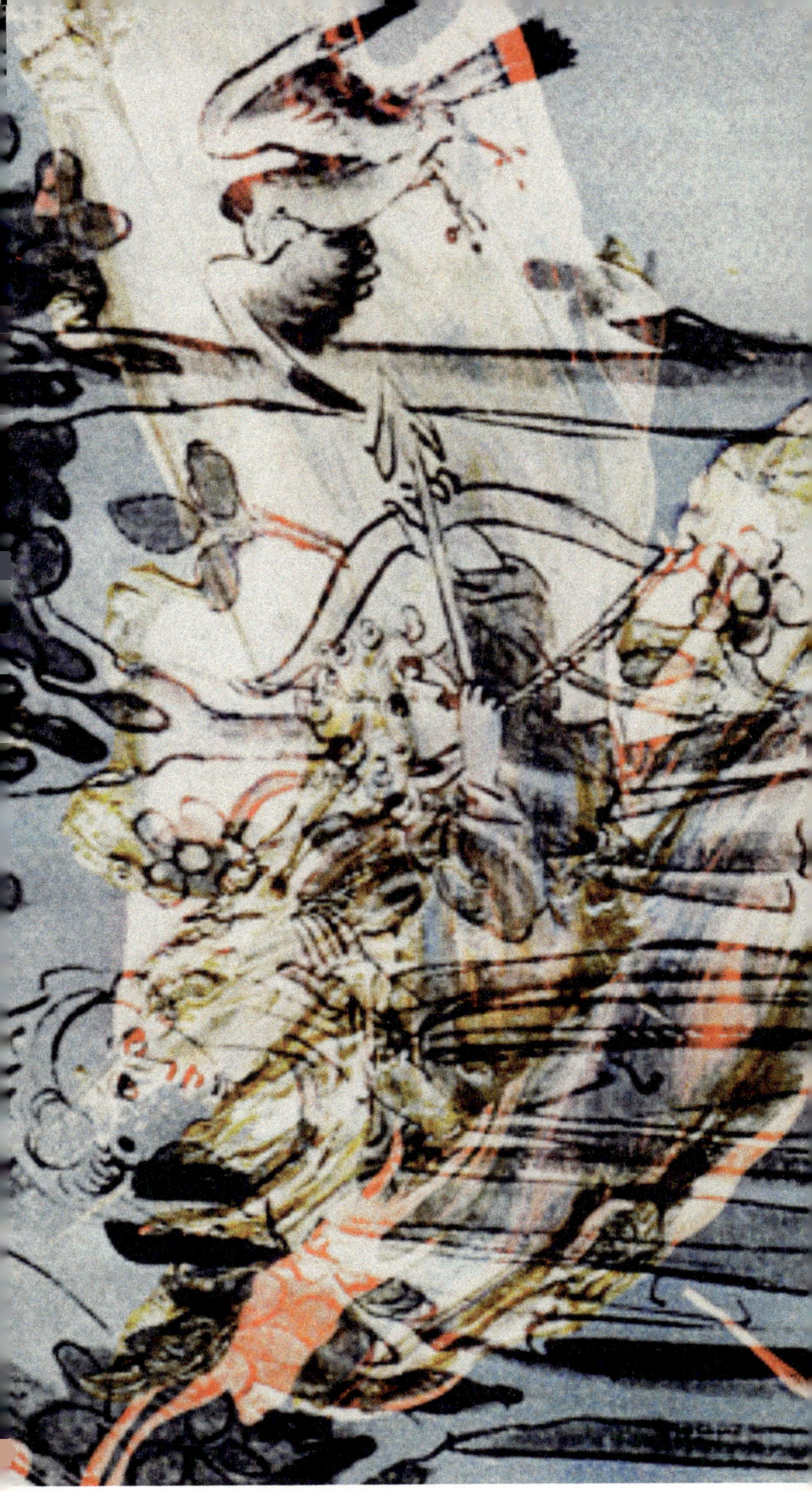

Film still from *Parsifal verlernen* (Unlearning Parsifal), 2018

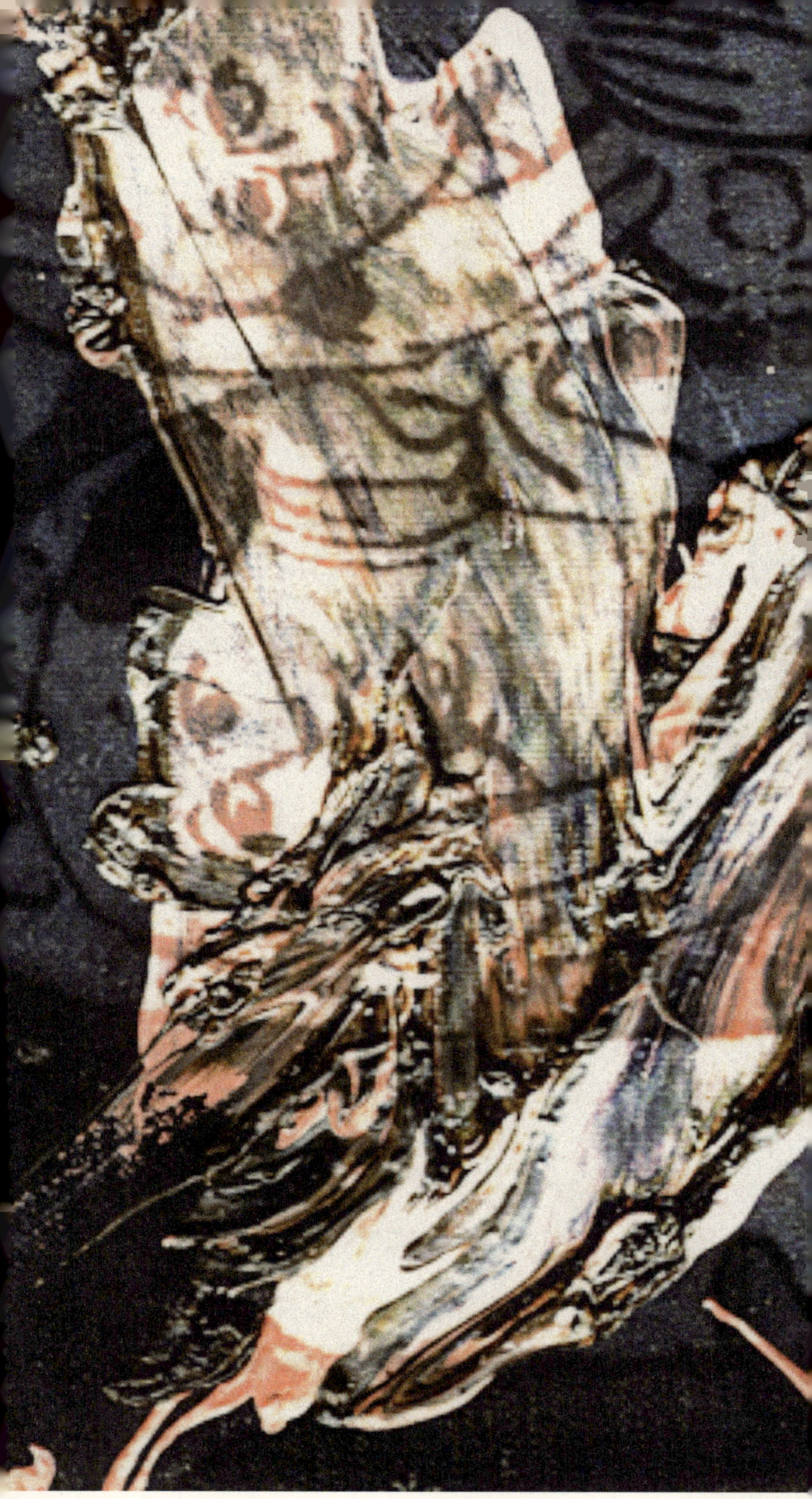

Film still from *Parsifal verlernen*
(Unlearning Parsifal), 2018

any
criticism of
her son”

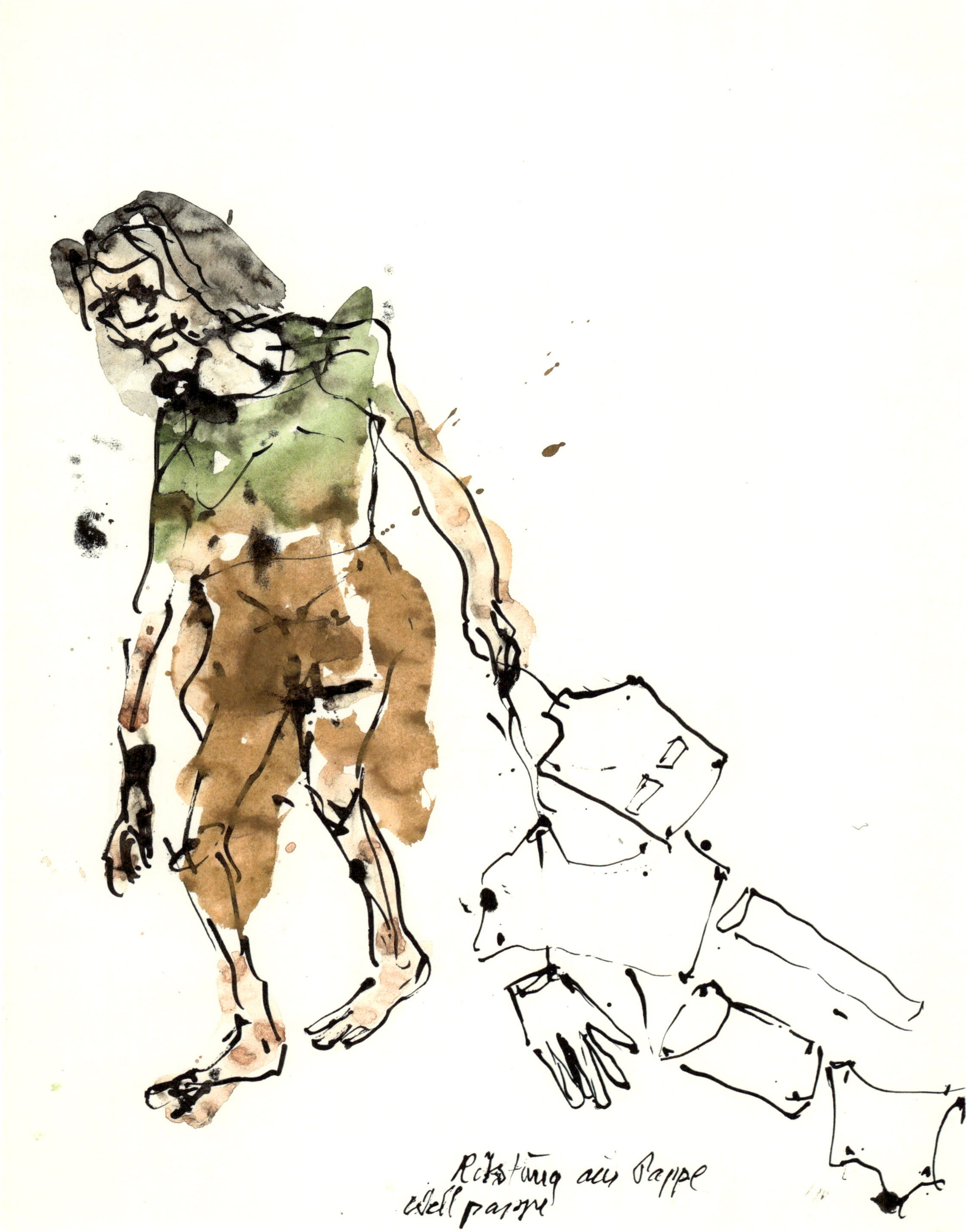

Armor made from cardboard, corrugated cardboard (Parsifal) 2017

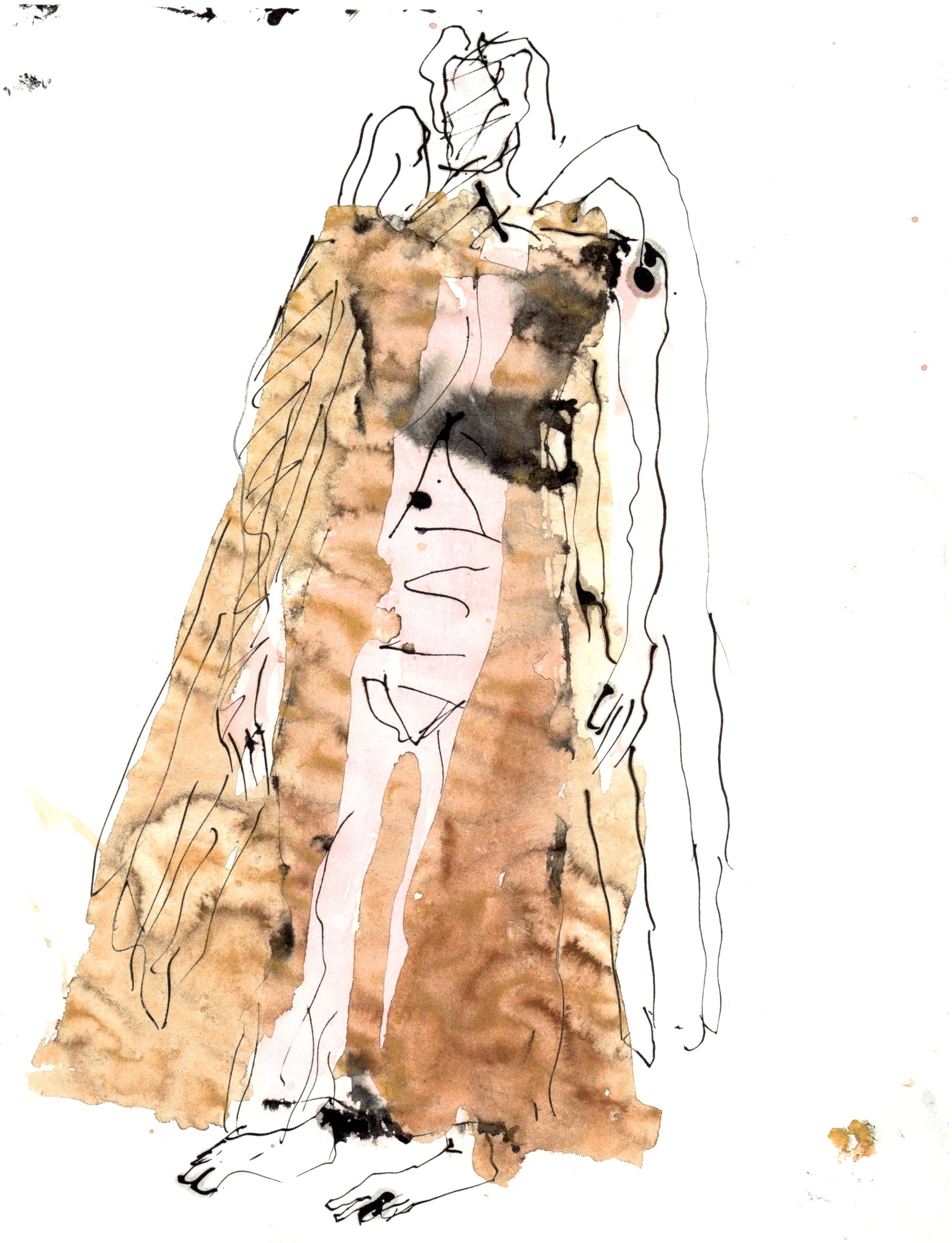

2017 Angel

THE LIMITS OF MOTHER WIT. MOTHER WIT IS CONTAGIOUS

Alert presentiment, always two steps ahead of her little son's stumbles. Herzeloyde's hand already reaches out. But doesn't grab him. The boy has to fall down, make his own mistakes. She'd been way ahead of every foolish thing her beloved Gahmuret did. Each morning she already knew what miscellany of nonsense, "deeds," damage to third parties she'd take note of late that afternoon. She cleared plenty of enmity out of her knight's path. She was generous by nature. Wit comes from abundance. "When the heart is full, wit leaps into the eyes." She worked exuberantly to POUR mother wit into Parsifal, who was all she had left besides her farm, farmhands and animals.

"Dear child, come here, but light no light
Where art thou? There! Thy teeth are out of sight!
Without thy voice thou art not so beguiling
But handsome enough to set my heart to smiling."

Herzeloyde had no clear image of what was right. She merely sought to ward off what was wrong. So what she gave the clever boy was not a complete understanding, but rather particles of her caution to take with him on his way (and she didn't even mean for him to set out on his way, but rather stay with her). She sewed him a fool's motley. That was meant to protect him from the worst, make him unsuited for the slick world out there. It's hard to transfer such a STOCKPILE OF UNDERSTANDING, and impossible when it's ambivalent.

WHEN PARSIFAL LEFT HER, HERZELOYDE'S MOTHER WIT WAS SPENT

The blithe spirit couldn't live without wit, and without her darling. When he left her, she died on the spot. In Chretien de Troyes, we see Parsifal heading off, turning around one last time, watching his mother collapse and continuing on his way. "No hay caminos, hay que caminar." In Wolfram von Eschenbach, Parsifal doesn't witness his mother's death. Years later he learns that his departure had meant the death of Herzeloyde was killed by his departure.

If Herzeloyde's mother wit ran dry, never touching Parsifal any more than it had touched the knight Gahmuret, what remains of it in this epic? It took root in the two poets (Chretien des Troyes, Wolfram von Eschenbach). Far below the black and white of ink on parchment or the clashing hues of a magpie's feathers flows groundwater that never runs dry: the "slanting gaze," the clairvoyant eye. In the solitude of Soltane, that mother wit would enter Herzeloyde's mind mostly in the morning hours, appearing in the background of her eyes. The eyes would gain a brightness they didn't always have.

THE CHILD OF A MEMBER OF THE WOMEN'S FLAK AUXILIARY

The only child soared on the wings of his mother's imagination. Utterly spoiled, he later led a group of activists that declared war on the world. A West German police task force dragged him, severely wounded, out of the garage where he'd taken cover on the run.

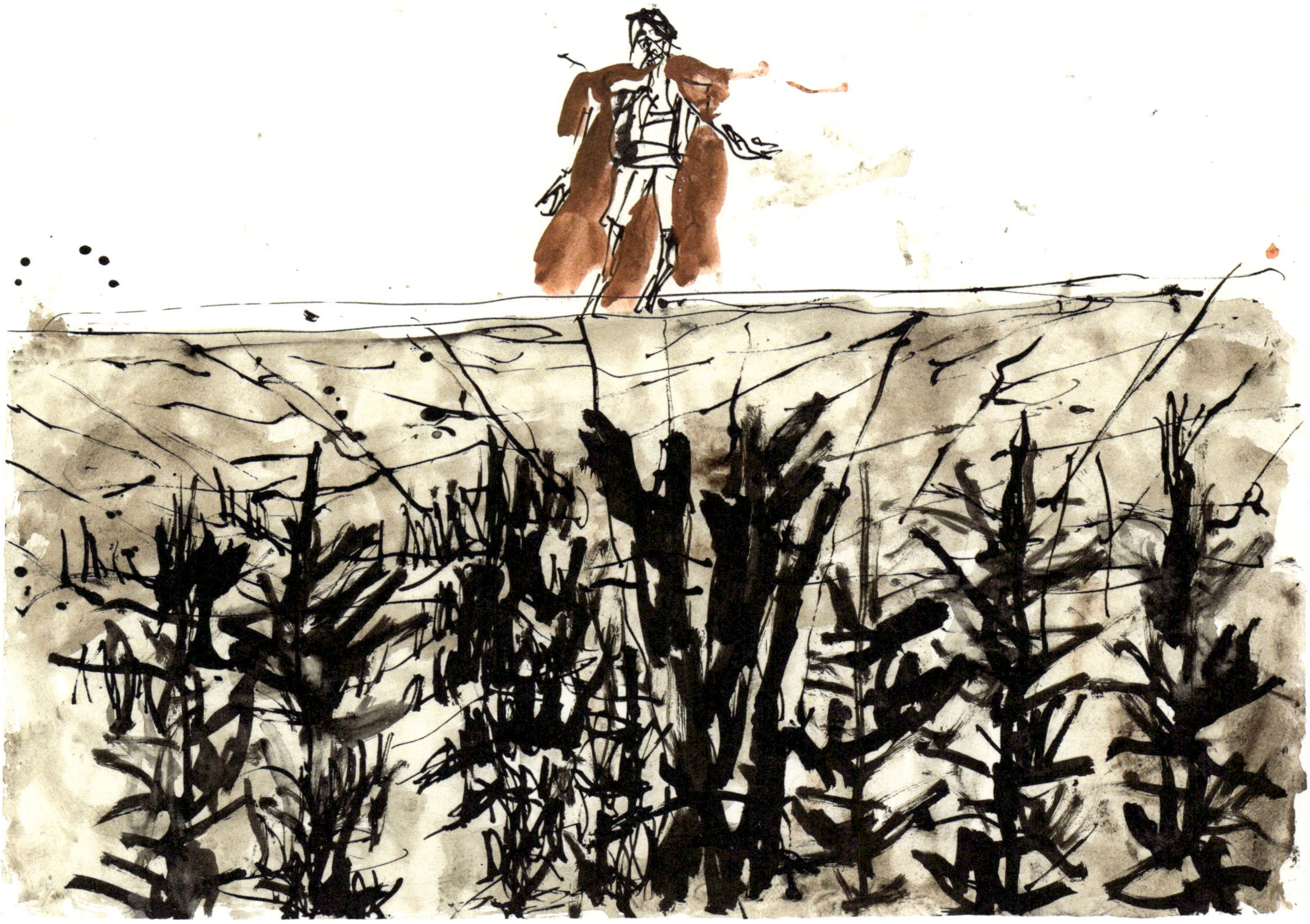

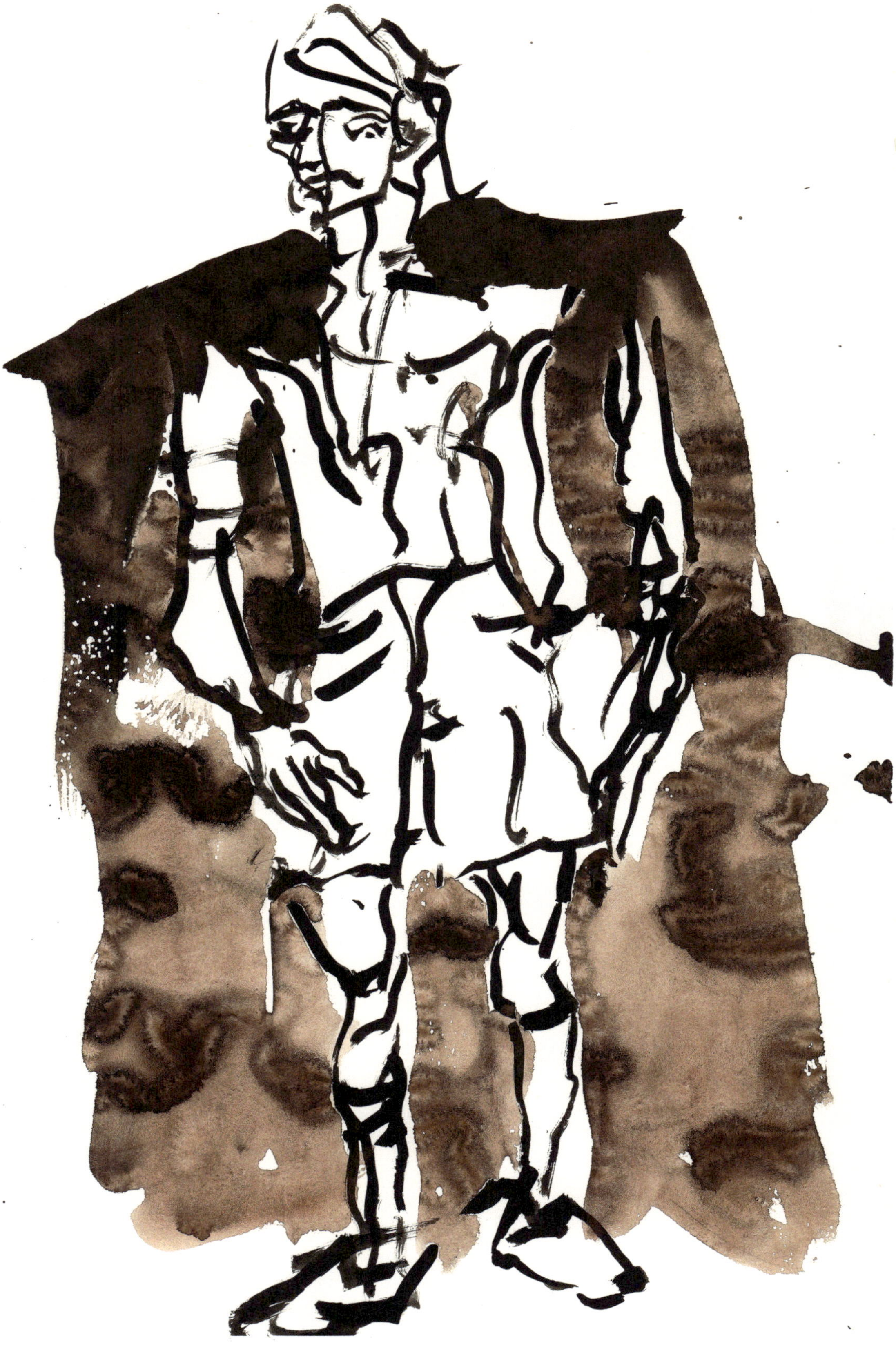

2017 Parsifal

The word "mother"
in colloquial German.

Mother
(in mining terminology):
"a lode, conceived as
soluble and ore-forming"

Mother
(in technical terminology):
the threaded hole into
which a bolt is inserted

"The mother of all winds
is the cold alone"

“However great the
mother’s need /
her child a warm meal
will she feed”

“Flutter, flutter
round the fount /
little mortal dragonfly /
round thy grave
and motherland”

“Mother dear,
leave me be / I shall live
by my own will”
(Parsifal)

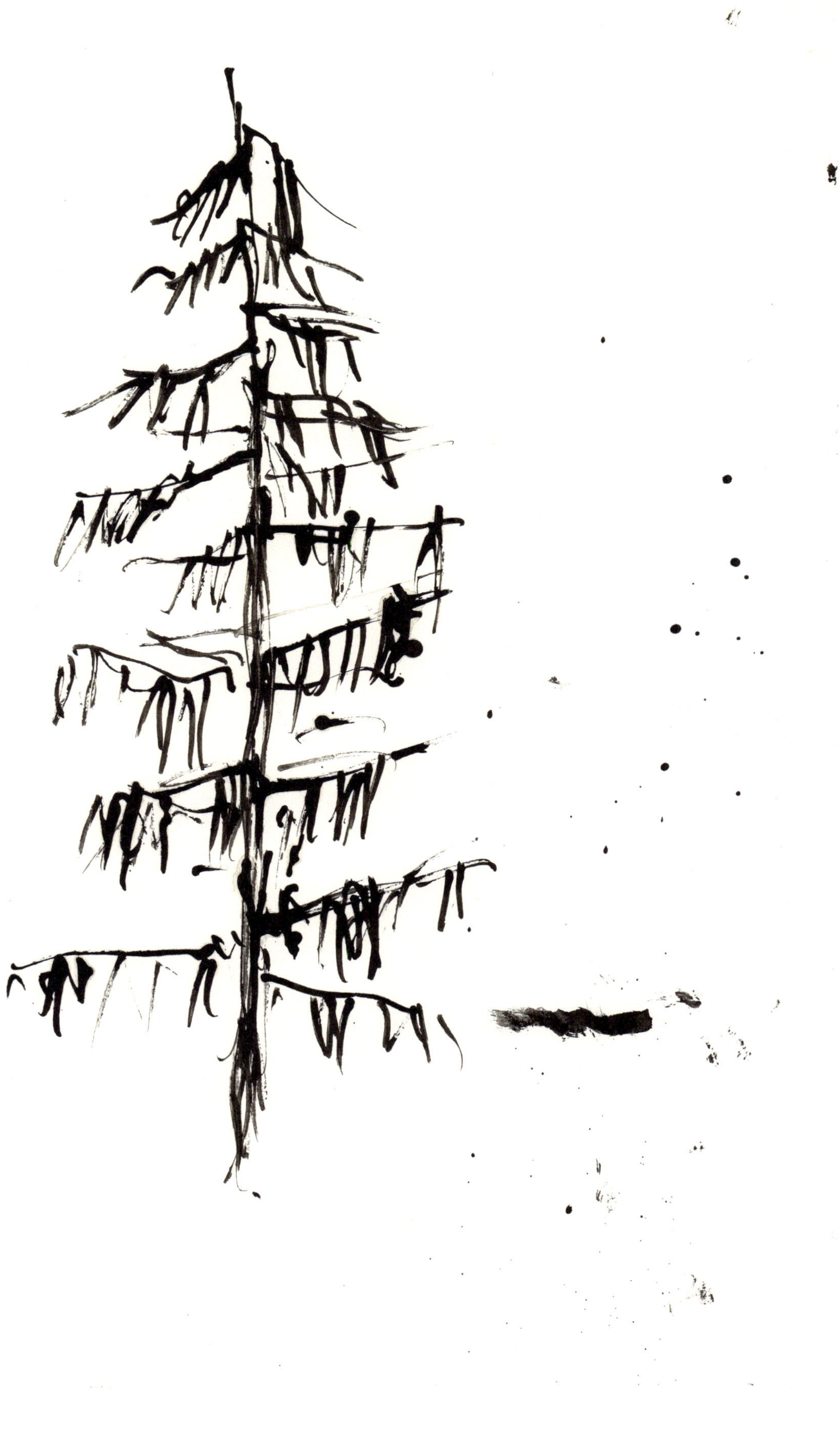

2017 Fir tree

“The opposite of mother wit is stingy soul”

American troops had reached Gröningen and Oschersleben and pressed on to Magdeburg. On April 12 the old woman left her farm in Langenstein, after feeding the cattle, and cycled to Ballenstedt. Her aim was to get her grandson out of the National Political Institute of Education (*Napola*) and take him home with her.

Just three years before, the opportunity for him to be educated at the *Napola* had struck her as a positive thing. She'd approved of the way farmer's children at the primary school were being selected for an academic high school and then transferred from there to the *Napola*. That would mean a good career path for a farmer's son. But that exclusivity now struck her as risky. And she couldn't bear the thought that a front line of hostile troops lay between her grandson (all that she had now that his father had fallen in battle and his mother had moved away from the farm) and herself. She didn't want to lose her grandson.

She pictured herself going up and speaking to him. He'd be standing with his comrades, she figured. She'd walk up to him and ask him to come with her. But at once she saw that such an attempt would aim at the impossible. A boy standing in his comrades' midst can't be fetched home by an old woman; her grandson wasn't a mama's boy. Hanging back inwardly, she continued on her way.

In Ballenstedt she prowled around the building, which stood on a hill. She made it as far as the school director's outer office. What was she supposed to say? She learned from the porter that her grandson's class was training in a forest higher up in the hills. There she headed, pushing her bicycle, rucksack strapped across her narrow shoulders, to watch the line of armed boys at the forest's edge. She had found a place to watch where the group wouldn't notice her. Now at least she'd seen her boy.

Late that night she returned to the farm. She had crossed the front line two times.

THE COSTUME PARSIFAL'S MOTHER GAVE HIM, THAT HE REFUSED TO PART FROM EVEN AFTER HE'D TRAINED AS A KNIGHT

The fool's costume that Herzeloyde devised for her Parsifal was a "suit of armor made from cardboard and lettuce leaves." The leaves had to be replaced when they withered, and later she replaced them with pieces of quilted down. The boy didn't know what hit him. Medieval illustrations depict the fool's costume incorrectly, like the sort of thing worn by Till Eulenspiegel. In fact, Parsifal's get-up was more similar to the camouflage worn by present-day paratroopers. Motley garb.

"... general and innate rules of understanding (possession of which is called mother wit) ..."

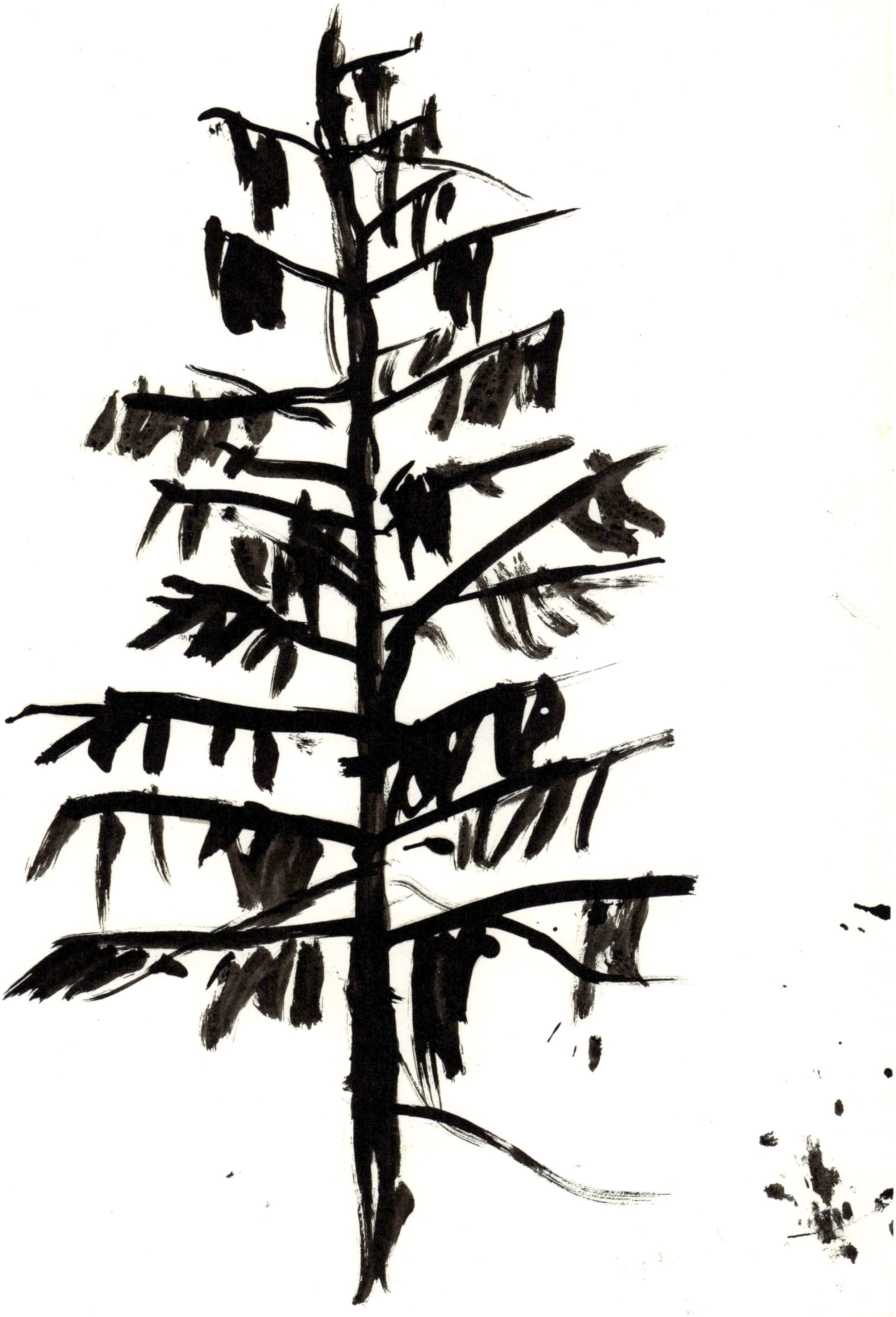

2017

Fir tree

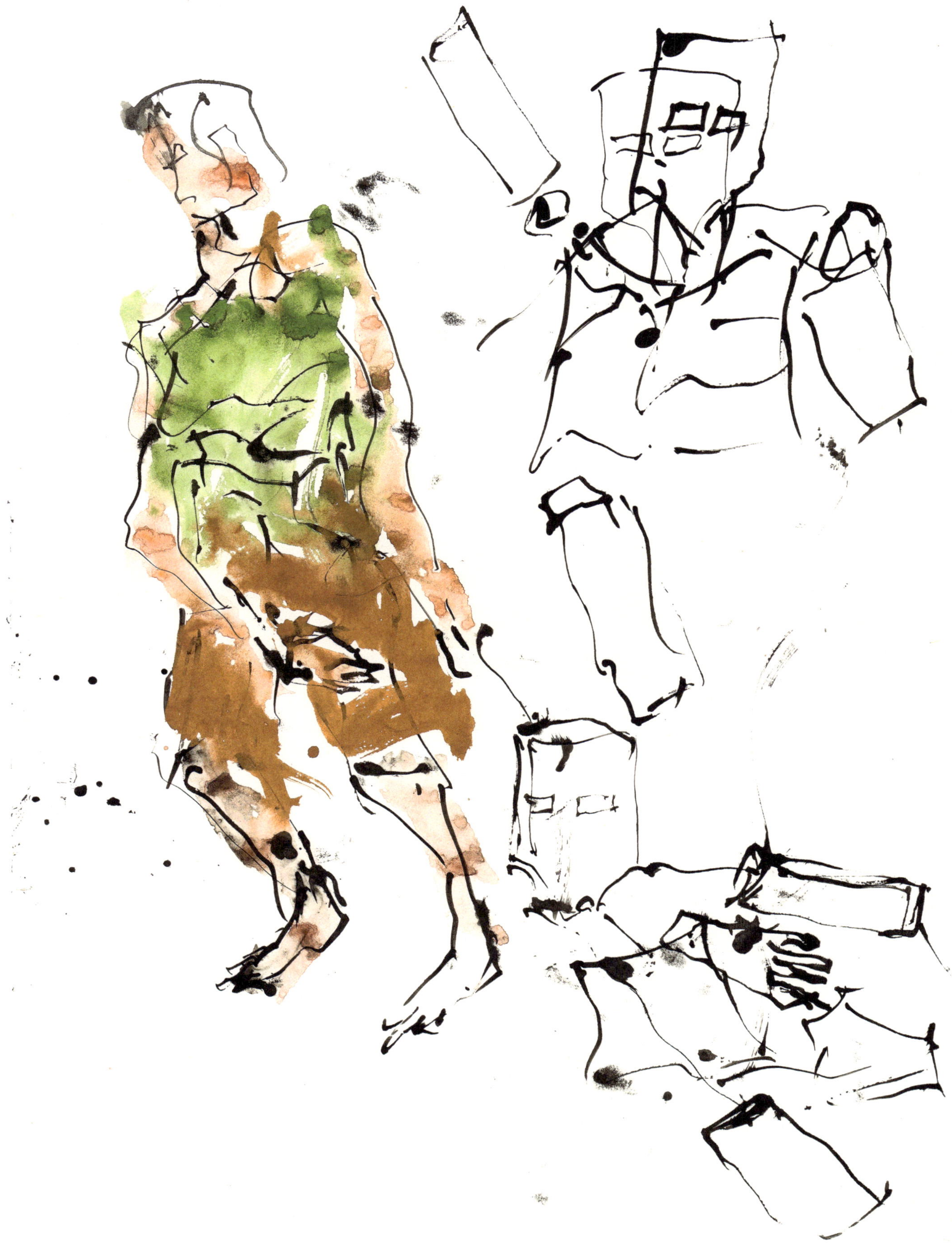

2017

Parsifal

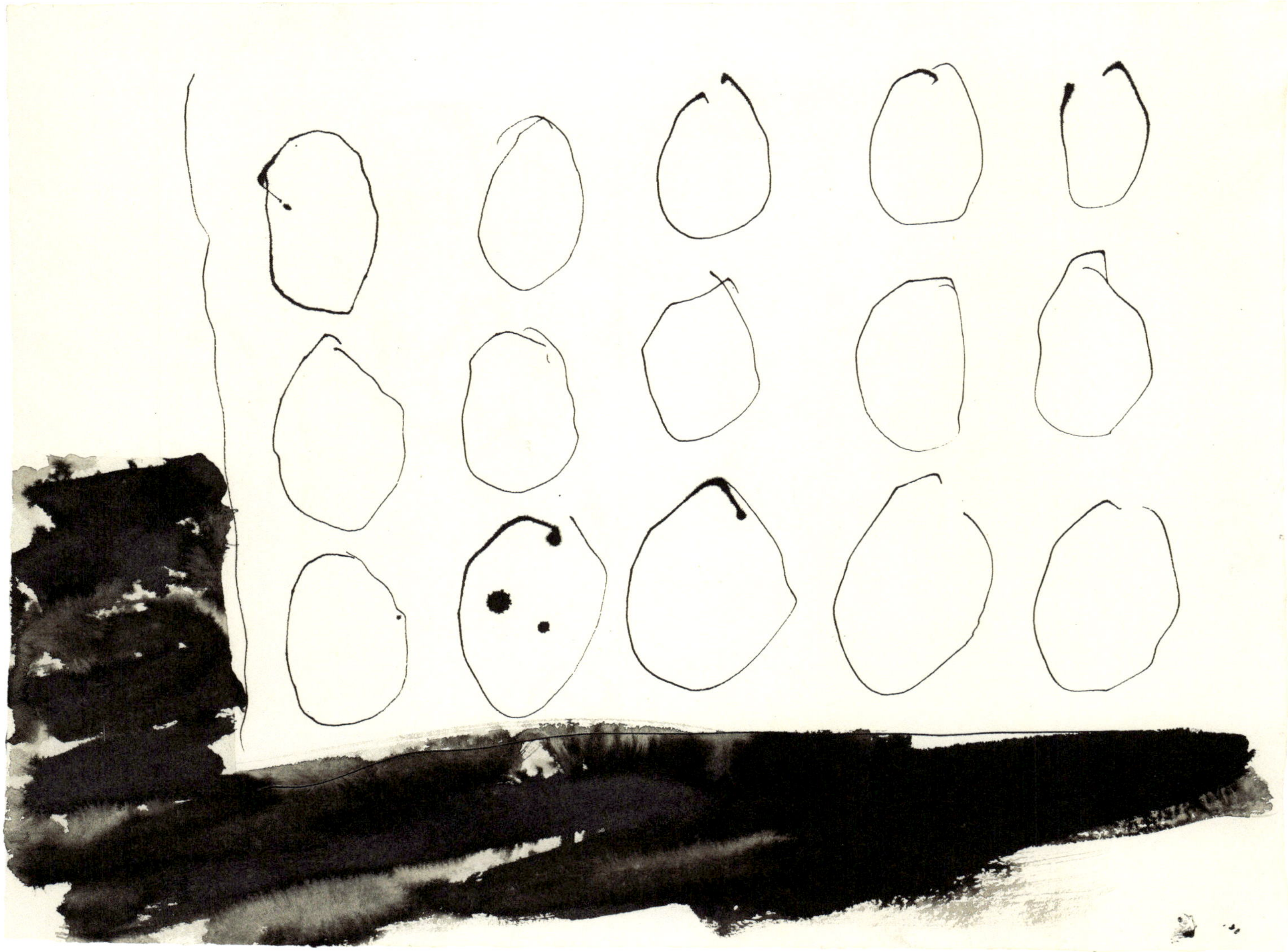

Set design, rejected

2017

He ran the American troops' supply depot. With his sense of the important things in life, he expanded the canteen to include seven brothels for the enlisted men and two for the officers. He was said to be a master at the art of seduction (France's reign had ended, he had remained), but he had given it up for the more powerful force of mammon. He couldn't personally escort the flower of girlish youth to each officer, nor the leftover second tier to the enlisted men. A web of money had to replace that supervision. Money is a faithless, mindless ruler, with little sensitivity for the uniqueness of some of the whores or the special personalities of their military johns, who often hailed from odd places in the heartland of the USA. The result was ejaculations without fascination, nothing for which a front-line soldier would want to stake the last thing he had, his life. The troops wavered. Bodily nourishment alone produces no victors.

"TRUST NO RENOWN PROCLAIMED BY WOMEN ..." MESSAGE FROM THE EASTERN FRONT, 1942

Objective: sector bounded right hand forest ravine north Schernovez—ravine—west slope elevation 324.8, bounded left hand chicken farm kolkhoz Bykovska—reach east slope up to elevation 213.4 ... in other words, the commanders who had issued the order demanding that this position be *reached* assumed that no enemies were present there. They were to march into this sector or ride in on motorcycles. Then, toward one in the afternoon, it turned out that they were riding into an inferno. The motorized advance guard radioed back to ask if the orders still stood. Yes, the reply came, the sectors were to be *taken* ("take" meaning "use force, attack"), and so the men rode on into a shredding machine that horribly wounded the young lieutenant Percy von Löhlein. How, years later, was he supposed to bring forth from that body's spirit the will to get through medical school examinations? How was he supposed to get through at all?

But his mother wouldn't have liked it if he had been a coward. She had released him from her protection, *consigned* him to school, *submitted* him to military service, *advised* him to volunteer, and even here, at the gates of Hell, she was at his side (as a motherly ghost), to cheer him on, kind-faced. She was weak when it came to the demands that the world placed on Percy, her representative appendage. And so she tossed her young Löhlein into that hellfire *proclaiming his renown*, ignorant in a different way than the deputy division commander Sörgel, who was unaware of the plight in the sector which the enemy was bombarding with masses of metal, and who therefore did not *feel* his culpability for this annihilation of an entire battalion.

It took five hours to transport Löhlein to the field hospital; as opposed to one and a half seconds from start to finish of the work of destruction in his body. That was the time it took for a piece of shrapnel to have its effect. The doctors found: a wound as from a cleaver, severing the 5th to 12th ribs near the spine. Each rib was cut in two, the abdominal cavity was open. A rib shard had lacerated one kidney and one lung. On the road Löhlein had "acted excited," "felt unwell"; he was given two and a half grams of sodium amytal, a sedative. He felt no pain. Senior doctor B.'s conclusion: *Pain loses control once the damage is too great*. In such cases we observe a collapse of the bonds of trust on which all messages between body and spirit depend. As he lay there rather impassive, but restless, they patched him together in makeshift fashion, without administering anesthetics, as they had none.

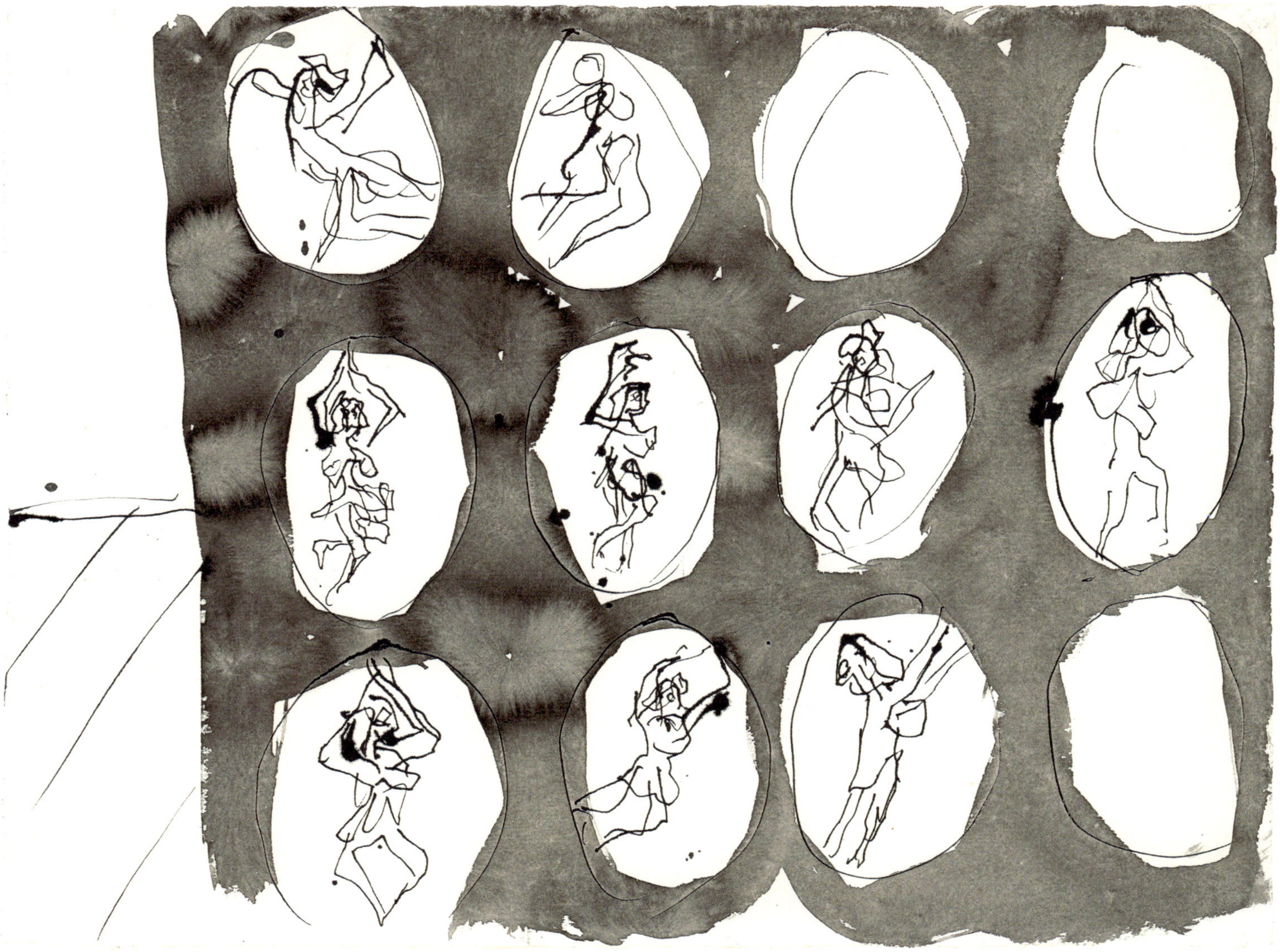

2017

Set design, rejected

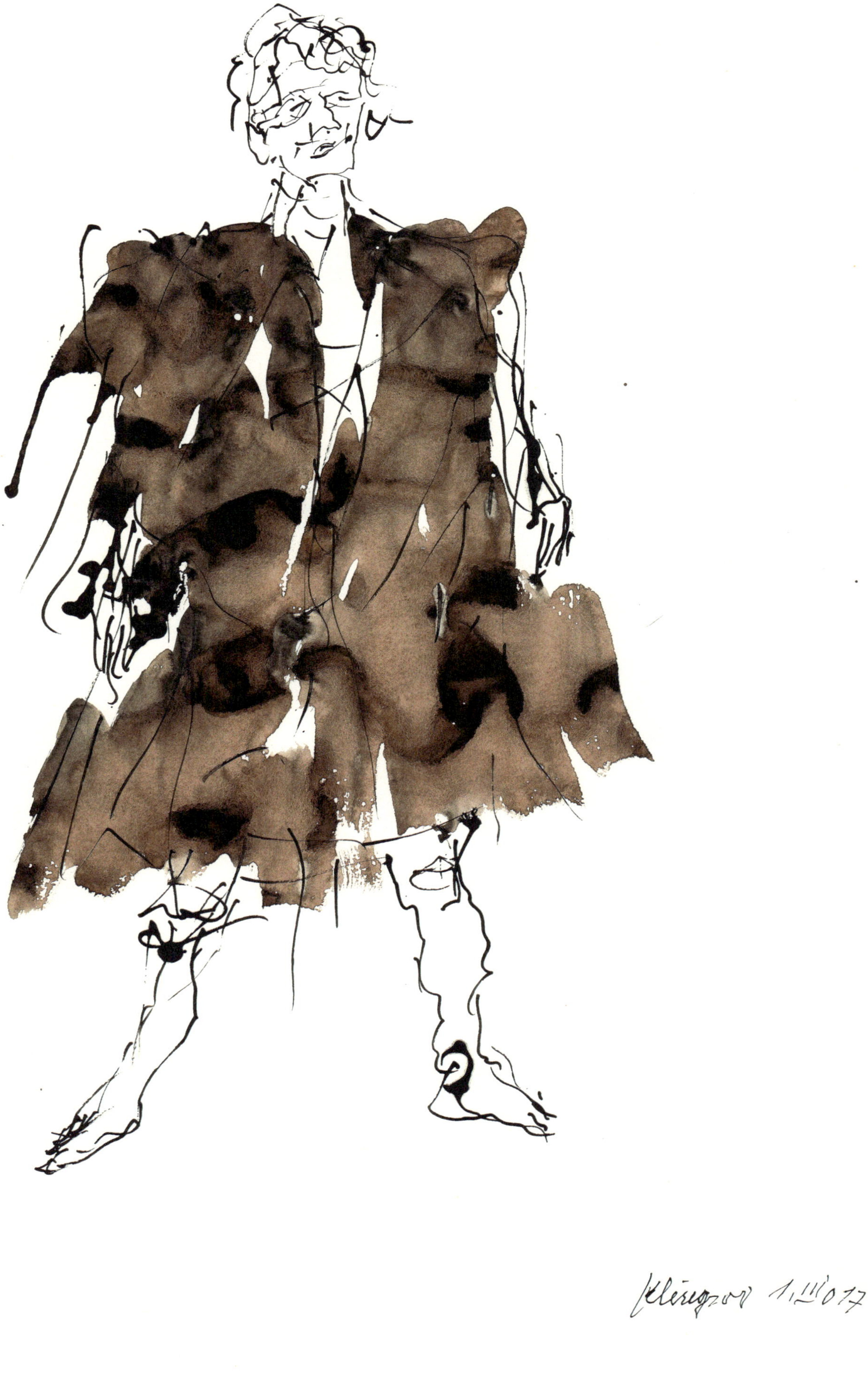

2017

Klingsor

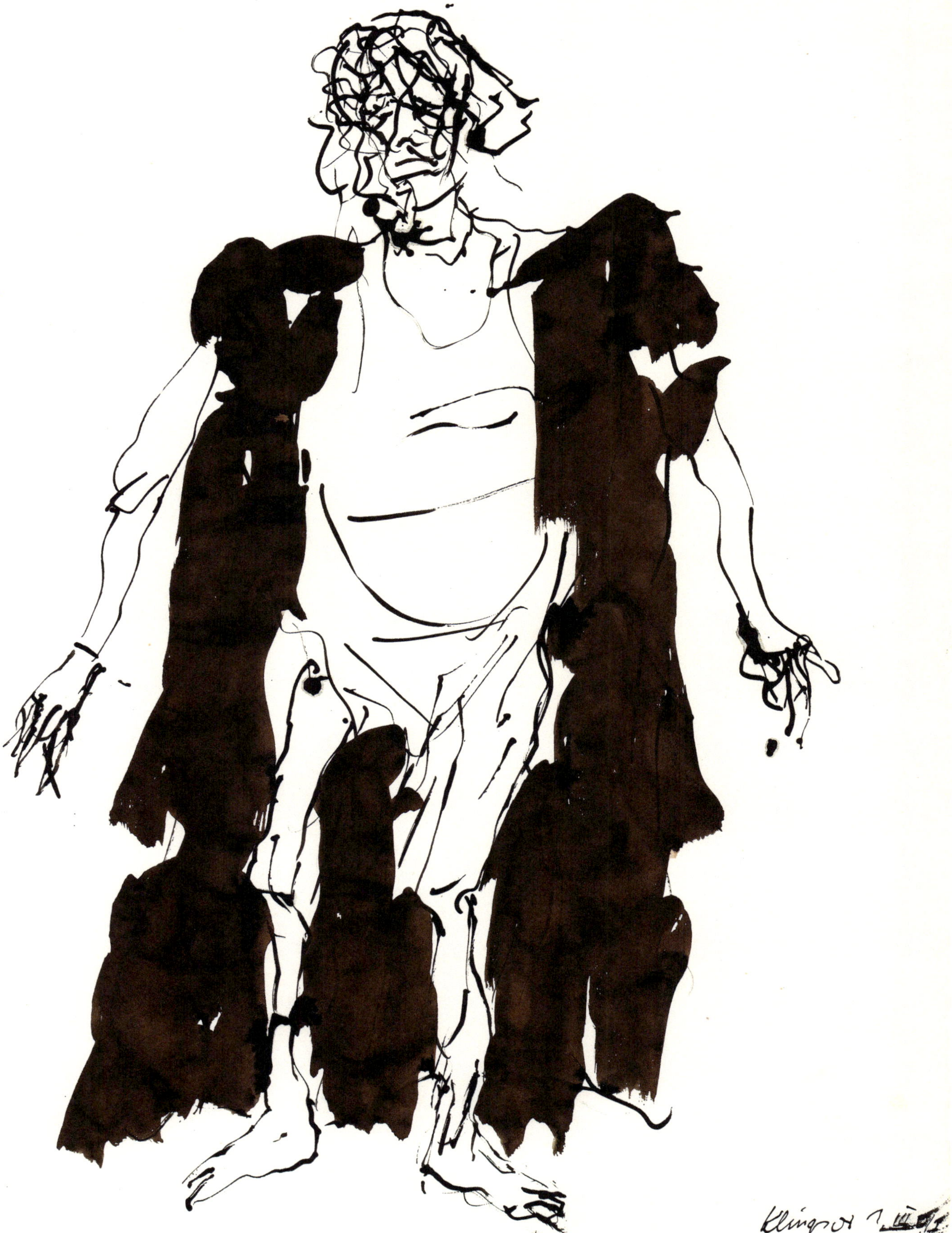

A good-for-nothing of a man won Anni W.'s heart in Bad Schlangenbad in the Taunus Mountains, where she was cleaning rooms in a hotel and helping out in the kitchen. He had "picked her up." Then the couple moved to a town in Central Germany, north of the Harz Mountains, where she worked for various households to support her work-averse husband and herself. Soon children came along. He cultivated his unemployment status from 1929 till late in 1933. Then he was forcibly recruited for an armament factory. Pressed into the ranks of an aircraft factory's work-force. In his work brigade he hardly did a stroke of manual labor, serving more as an advisor and best buddy, and lending a hand with simple tasks. Mainly he provided his colleagues with girls in their spare time. He was popular.

Though he was earning his own wages now, little of his pay ended up in Anni W.'s household. And he came home late, too. She kept the children fed, first her oldest boy, then two daughters; a third was adopted by a kindhearted neighborhood family. Anni herself consumed very little. A thin, quick person. Meanwhile she had given birth to her fourth child in the marriage with the work-shirker. Her oldest boy was her helper in the line of duty. Now it was wartime. All-round workers like Anni W. were needed. These were her glory days. She was working for the last child she would carry in her belly: Oskar, to be her favorite.The moment the bundle was placed in her arms, she knew that this youngest child would be the dearest thing on earth to her.

Early on she had imprinted her firstborn with the persuasiveness inherent to the permanent will to work, the absolute dedication to others. She made him her emissary. In the Middle Ages one would have said *her sword*; now you'd have to call him "her third hand," pillar of the family republic. This way she could afford her beloved youngest son as well as the flighty fellow whom, however useless he was in practice, she'd loved and grown used to ever since Bad Schlangenbach. In the meantime she'd had an operation. On doctor's orders. She was not available for further pregnancies. She went on working non-stop so that everyone could get by. This woman's dark energy glowed in her sons as well.

Meanwhile the family had survived World War II. In the Soviet Zone of Occupation, later the Workers' and Farmers' Republic, Anni W.'s underprivileged status became a badge of honor. Many a high-ranking functionary would have been glad to have the resumé she boasted. Both her sons studied at the program for workers' and farmers' children at the University of Halle. The youngest went on to become mayor of a city; the oldest was an engineer, a factory manager, by the Republic's 40th year a high-ranking cadre in an industrial ministry. Both were the opposite of their father as far as their relationship to work was concerned.

In a "thousand-year Reich of socialism," these two "Knights of Labor," emissaries of their hardworking mother, would have been honored to their dying day and beyond as honorary citizens of a REPUBLIC OF LABOR. But that was not to be. When the Berlin Wall came down, the Republic had lasted a mere forty years. The proportion of planned economy and administration had been much too high to suit Marx's ideal of a Republic of Labor. Thus, one brother became an affluent citizen of the West, while the other still carries the Republic in his heart, twice a year riding his own motorcycle to his retirement dacha in Spain.

EXPANSION OF A CHILD'S SOUL INTO VASTNESS

With her unborn son "under her heart" (though presumably the child had already slipped farther down), "Klara with the bright eyes," the later Frau Hitler, for now merely a woman pregnant out of wedlock, lay abed on the ground floor of the house. On the second floor the child's father's legitimate wife lay dying. Twofold disgrace: that the woman upstairs was dying, and that Klara's pregnancy would remain secret and illegitimate so long as that woman was alive. Klara held firm to her refusal to wish the wife upstairs a speedier death.

What Klara "thought" at a profoundly subliminal level in the twilit hours of those nights and days imparted itself (in a manner no clinical test could reconstruct) to the boy whose diapers she was changing in his crib a few weeks later. The young soul absorbed his mother's mission through the pores of his skin: a royal mother must never again lie in disgrace. Decades later, even after a brief training as a propaganda speaker on military policy by officers of the Bavarian regiment where he'd been transferred after his stay in the military hospital, his speechless soul confused the humiliation of the beloved mother—which he felt predestined to avenge—with the manifest HUMILIATION OF GERMANY. His initial oratorial outbursts, resulting from the confusing and mixing of the two messages, met with great acclamation at the propaganda evenings he was commanded to hold. There was an undertone in the speaker's words that immediately fired up his listeners. Between 1919 and 1923 a "pattern of subversive persuasion" thus formed in the youthful Hitler—indispensable for a propagandist, fed by a spring from an earlier world. Inside, the quiet, rather inarticulate soul of the mother-warrior was joined by a rhetorical force, retrievable at will, that was rather alien to Klara's soft soul. Or wasn't the maternal soul so soft and thin-skinned after all? A white soul-horse was harnessed inside the young orator, providing the traction. That set the tone. Whereas the other part of the soul, a black horse with rolling eyes, determined the force. The two parts of the soul ran side by side. Since one of them was an artificial beast, born of misinterpretation, its "muscles" could withstand a strain beyond all natural bounds. They could enter the race with the force of copper or steel, "focused" or "overstretched." That was what adjutants, observing Hitler at close hand, later referred to as the Führer's will (his "unbridled willpower").

THE COSTUME OF KLINGSOR THE MIRACLE WORKER

"Duke Klingsor" is mentioned in the fifteenth book of Wolfram von Eschenbach's *Parsival* (Eschenbach, unlike Wagner, spells his Parsifal with a v). The poet speaks of the "cunning" Klingsor.

Sir, I shall tell you how he is
He did many people harm
The name of his land is Terra di Lavoro
He descends from a forefather
Who likewise worked many wonders:
Virgil of Naples...

How did this man become a sorcerer? Once, when he was furtively sleeping with the wife of a king, the ruler surprised him. The king's wife was lying snug and lovely in his arms.

For the warmth he found there
Klingsor made this forfeit:
Royal hands made him
Smooth between the legs

Having been castrated on that adventure (he wore a sling on one arm to distract from the actual location of the injury and was regarded as "wounded"), the knight had no choice but to become a sorcerer. That happened not in Persia, but in the city of PERSIDA, where he learned alchemy and the art of transformation (miracles & magic). Then he built Chastelmarveille (Old French for "Castle of Marvels").

Richard Wagner turned this supporting character from Eschenbach's epic into a brutal antithesis to the grail, a PROTAGONIST OF EVIL. The second act of Wagner's opera is devoted to him. The Klingsor act has dramatic, "modern" music. No matter how this middle part of *Parsifal* is staged, it remains mysterious. The set designed by Georg Baselitz reveals a gap leading inside Klingsor's miracle world—straight into the mystery.

Baselitz drapes Klingsor's shoulders in a short Roman military cape, the kind worn by the barracks emperors in ancient Rome. The legend of King Arthur, Wolfram von Eschenbach's source for the Klingsor character, assembles the debris of ancient tales. What connects the (evil) Klingsor with the poet Virgil? Eschenbach names Virgil as Klingsor's forefather. What is demonic about the art of poetry? Art is never harmless. Is that the root of Wagner's Klingsor? Is art's modernity merciless? Is there such a thing as the "gaping maw of modernity"? Who is Parsifal if he shuts that maw? In certain newer stagings, Klingsor reappears in the third act after dying in the second act. He oversees Kundry's death, twice as a witness, a third time as the executor. He takes part in the final meeting of the corps of volunteers who convene to drink from the grail.

Brazil, the USA, Russia, Italy, England, the northeast of France have recently seen an outbreak of "pustules on the skin of politics." The sociologist Richard Sennett speaks of authoritarian structures inserting themselves into reality. But wherever HEGEMONY establishes itself (auctoritas, imperium, violentia, vis), it is soon besieged by PRAETORIAN GUARDS. "Heroic guardians" who end up killing their wards. Rather than take the place of their victim, they elect one of their own as a new ward, whom they kill in turn later on. The character of Klingsor in the costume designed by Baselitz recalls a Roman Praetorian prefect. At night the Praetorian guards get drunk on a shared drink. The vessel is visible, the drink invisible, spiritual. The name of the potion they imbibe is: "Loyalty is my honor."

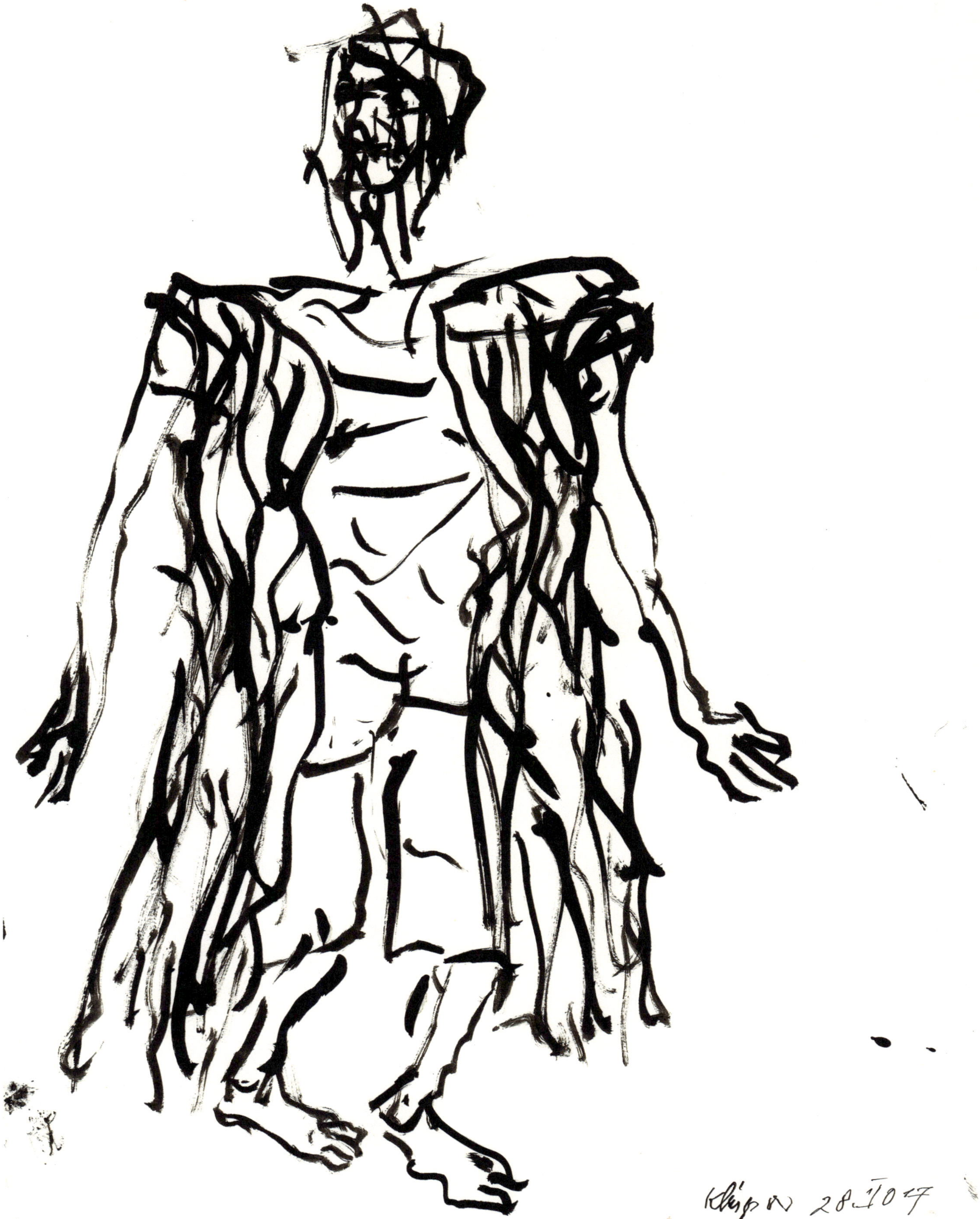

2017

Klingsor

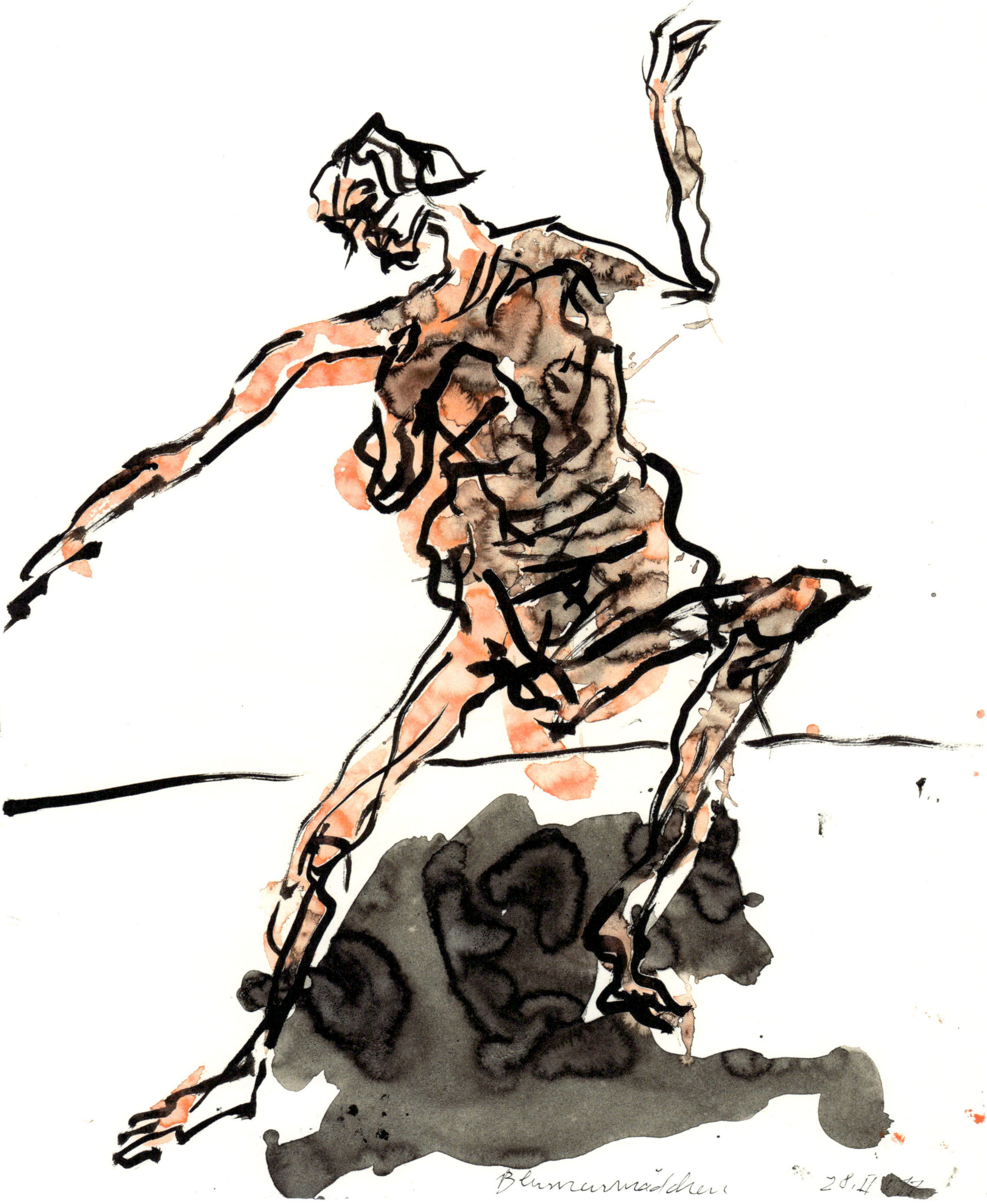

2017

Flower girl

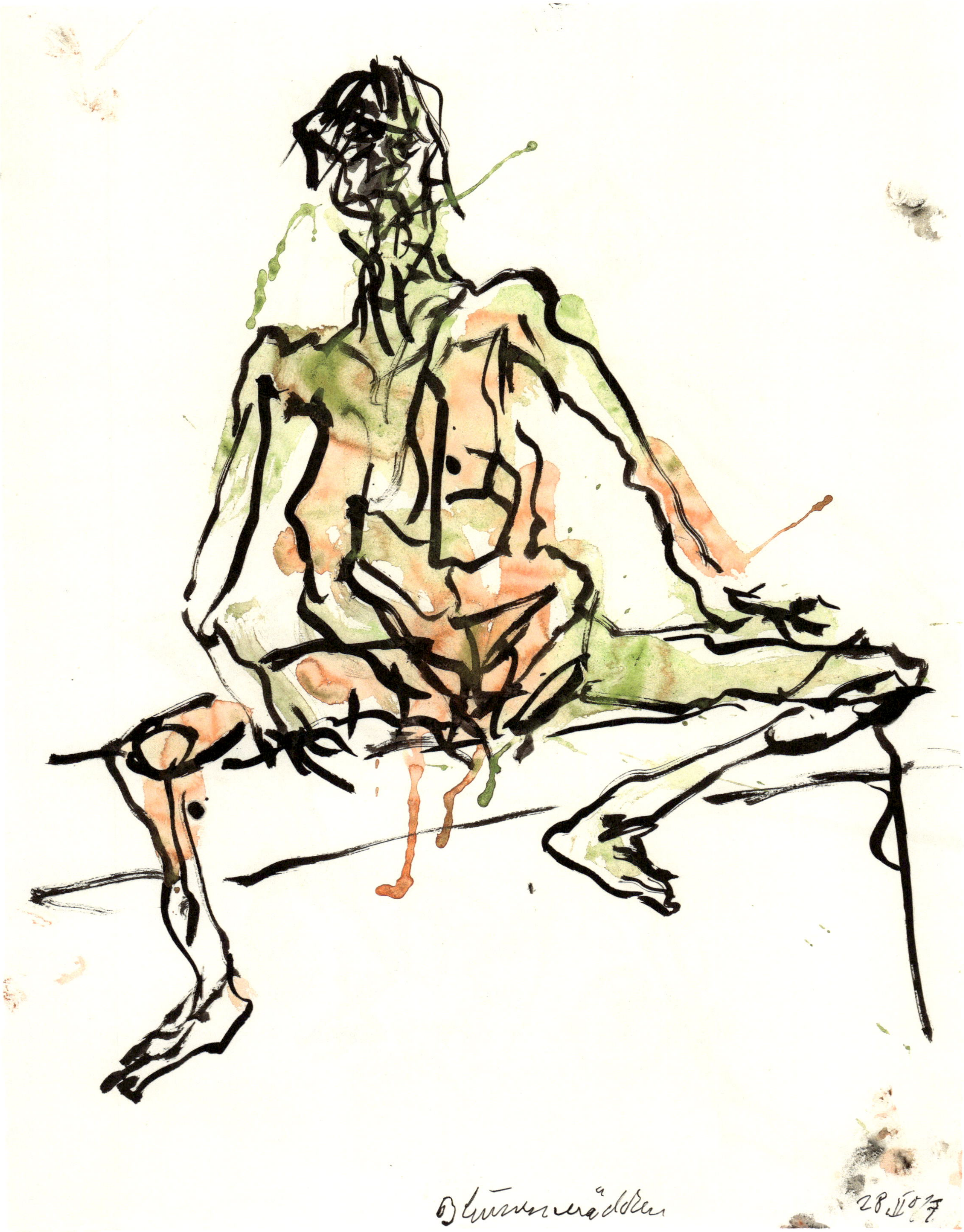

Flower girl **2017**

It's said that King Arthur gathered Britain's relevant warriors at his table lest their aggressiveness devastate the surrounding countryside. Now they sat at King Arthur's court as France's quarrelsome nobility would later sit at the court of Versailles, or Japan's daimyōs (lords) at the shogun's court—concentrated like prisoners in a magic castle. Thus begins the state's monopoly on the use of force, the only antidote to the butchery of civil wars. But even at the ruler's court, the knights of the Round table went on carrying their aggressive dreams in their heads. The idea of the grail, which King Arthur sent the heroes to quest for, served to discharge an excessive lust for fighting. And so they set out. Moved into the magic castle where the fool Parsifal chaired the meeting, at the new table, high up on the Mountain of the Holy Grail: what was the drink, the drug that animated them? According to Wagner, it was music. To *SS-Hauptsturmführer* Otto Rahn, the legendary Parsifal scholar, we owe the proof that the spiritual substance that emboldened and beguiled the grail's volunteer corps, imbibed not through the mouth but through the ears, is now scattered in droplets across the entire globe. This trace element of bellicosity can be detected in the aggressivity of its carriers that is instantly sparked by even tiny fractions of these droplets. It's absurd to use the word "percentage" in this context, speaking of quantities measured not in hundreds of parts, but in millions. If, instead of a percent, we use a "ratio of grail blood to mystery," we find 1.9 particles of grail blood in the veins of John Bolton, the security advisor fired by President Trump; 21.3 particles in Mussolini's kidnaper Dr. Skorzeny; and the enormous ratio of 31.2 particles in a project manager at the American Enterprise Institute, drafter of neo-conservative policy. Six weeks later, after being seduced by a young woman (a KGB agent) in a Washington apartment, the aggression level of the "grail-blooder" sank to 0.2. The intoxication of a warmonger contaminated by grail blood corresponds to an alcohol level of over 9 per mil in a motorist, for which reason grail-drunk characters cannot be permitted to navigate international politics.

"LANCING A POLITICAL FOLLY THE WAY YOU OPEN AN ABCESS"

It is a little-known fact that Hitler, after being blinded in a gas attack, was sent to a military hospital in Pasewalk and entrusted to a doctor with psychiatric training. The doctor's diagnosis: hysterical blindness. That is, not blindness by chemical irritation, nor from shock or cowardice (escape from reality). Rather, the cause was "an odyssey of the soul that has not yet found its destination." The doctor began with a psychoanalytic talk therapy. In the course of such a treatment, the patient develops a temporary dependency on the doctor. An aborted analysis is said to fix the soul in the state in which the treatment was abandoned. It is then crystallized as though in an in-between world.

The attending physician was a nationalist. He belonged to a *Freikorps*—a right-wing volunteer corps. With the revolutionary situation coming to a head, his comrades summoned him to Berlin, and the patient Hitler was left behind in Pasewalk with an unfinished therapy. Cured from his blindness—blinded by delusions.

In 1943, in the middle of World War II, a research group in the US secret service learned about the aborted therapy from statements by a German émigré in Iceland. The group was responsible for researching the German dictator's weaknesses. Even the power of the psyche must be deployed against the foe. The research group included followers of Sigmund Freud as well as a theoretician associated with the Institute for Social Research, which had moved from Frankfurt am Main to New York. They developed the plan to insert an experienced psychoanalyst into the inner circle of the German chancellor, so as to resume the treatment abandoned in autumn 1918 and "tame" the dictator to further the Allied fortunes of war. The operation failed because the group could find no one with sufficient psychological experience who was capable of being smuggled into the Führer's headquarters. At that point in the war the experts considered such a thing to be impossible.

A LOST SOUL CAN SET THE WORLD ON FIRE

A royal court like King Arthur's is filled with lots of people milling around each other: travelers, traders, bastards, aristocrats, farmers visiting their daughters, vassals. This leads to mix-ups when their souls make the leap into modern times. Once, a soul from the seventh century advanced to high political office. The soul, displaced in country and time, did not feel lost, far from it. To be sure of its reality it had to wrestle, touch others, be slandered, exchange ideas. Minute by minute it electrified its surroundings anew. Just as it strewed sparks from the quiver it had brought along from over 1500 years ago. Lots of hay in the world, easily flammable. In general, one should avoid piling up hay.

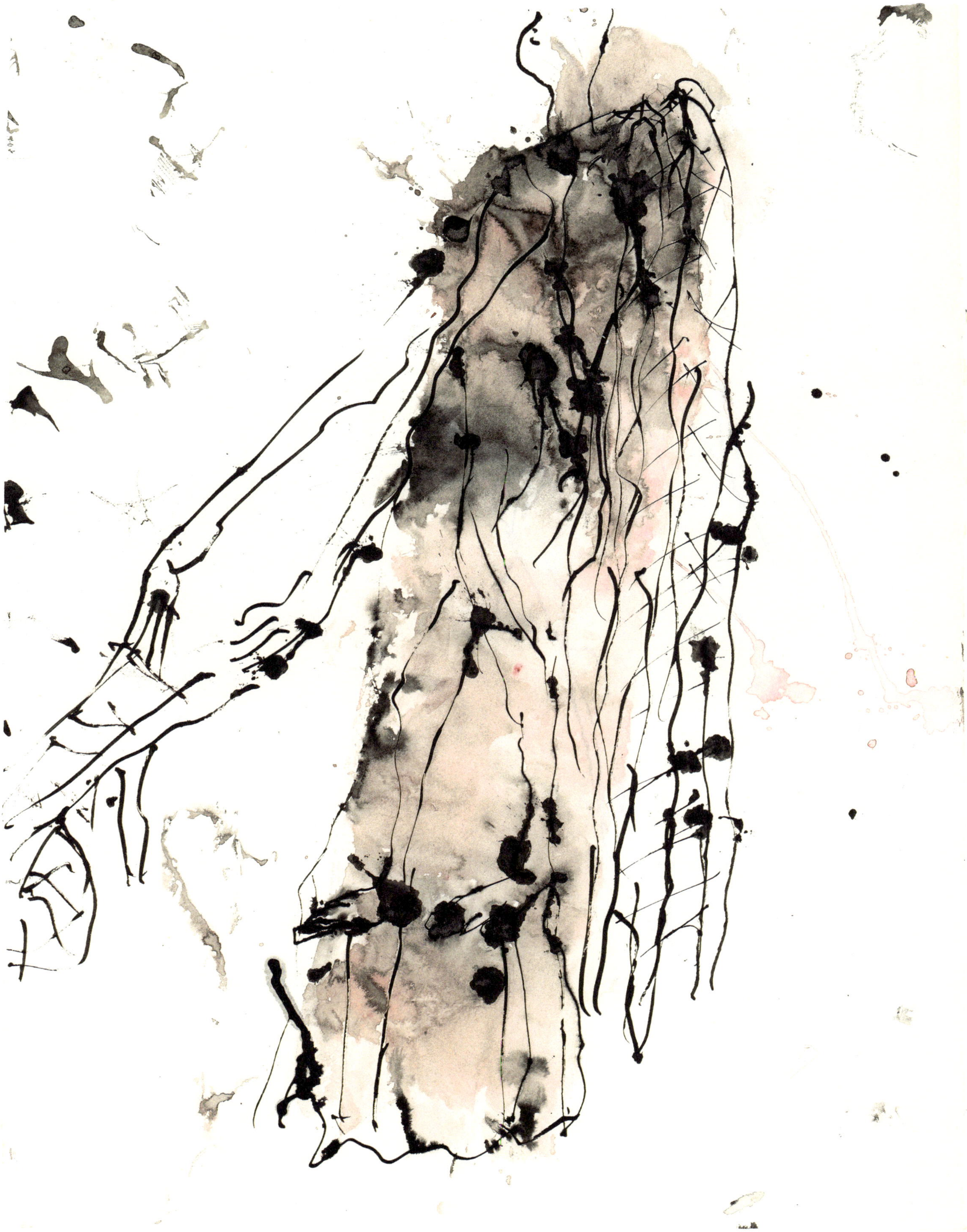

2017 Untitled

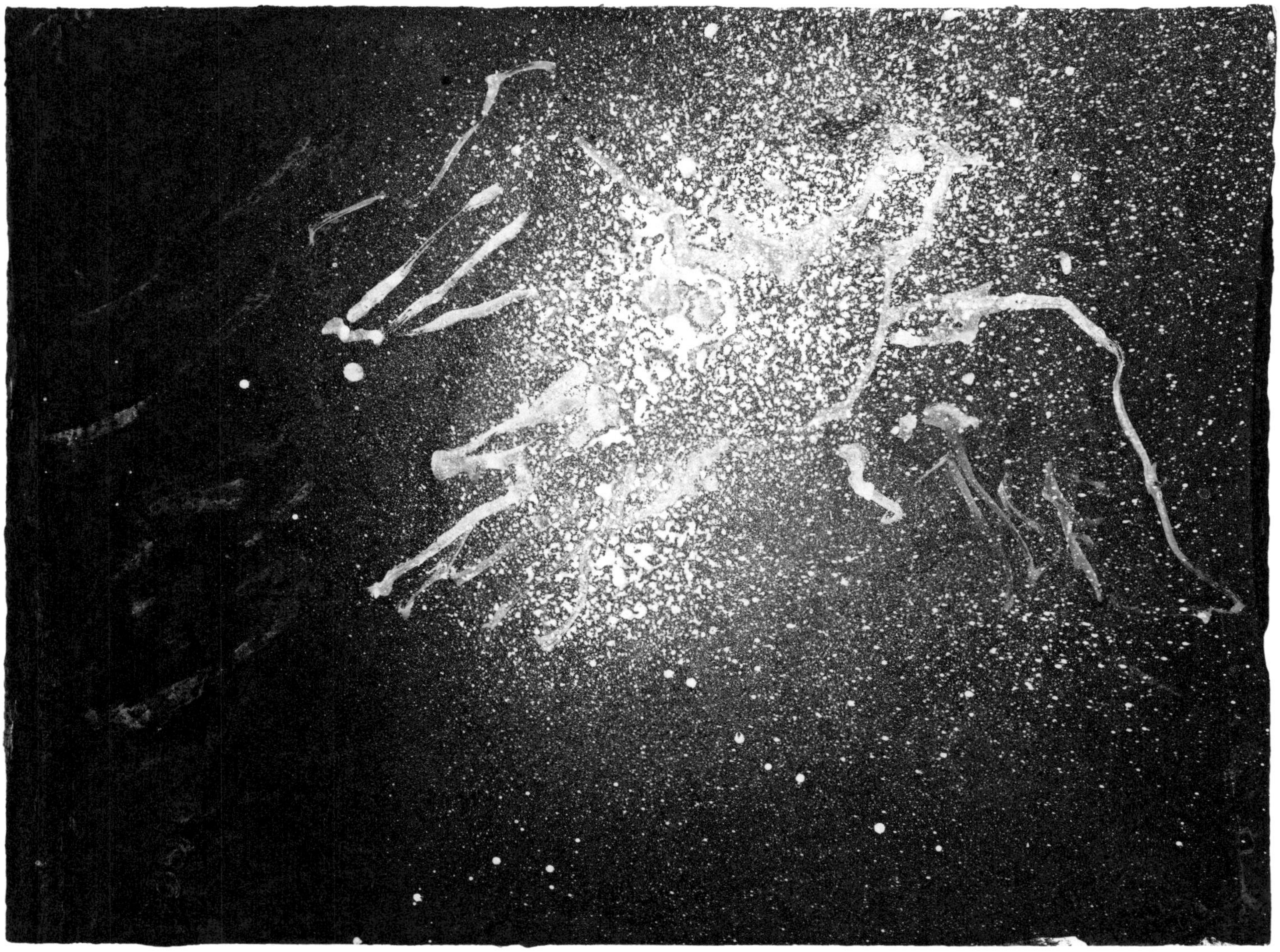

Curtain

2018

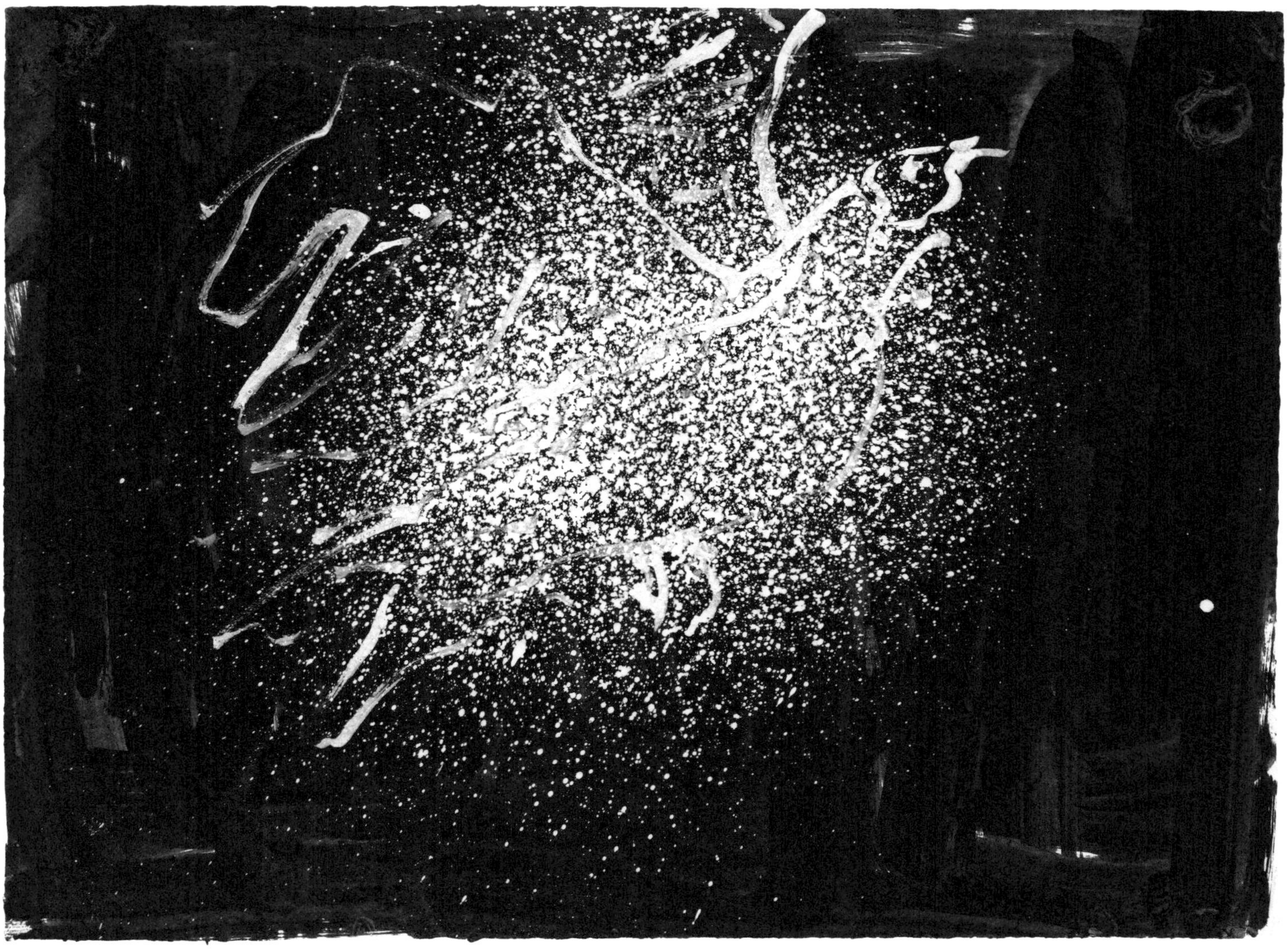

2018

Backdrop dove

Heiner Müller liked to cite Bert Brecht's words that the modern world has "slipped into the functional." Nothing material, nothing personal is real in itself; only the purpose makes it into a real thing—as when a uniform transforms a civilian into a soldier.

The century is dreaming. But the dream merely reshuffles the existing elements. For instance, the new Republicans from the Trump camp, courted as "emissaries from the New World" at the Munich Security Conference in 2017, were a type of American that had existed before, just one that was little known in Europe. By contrast, if things and people ever really do slip into the FUNCTIONAL, the result is a flood of refugees in rubber dinghies like those in the Aegean heading toward the IMAGINARY, the dimension that simply overruns all that is functional, vertical and horizontal. The sky and the horizons turn black. In the midst of a storm that beat down on him with such blackness and bolts of lightning, Martin Luther was transformed from a student to a prophet.

"HE HAD 25 ARMIES (EACH A DIFFERENT LANGUAGE!), AS BEFITTED HIS POWER."

One need not attribute any reflective consciousness to him, opening the door to the presidential bedroom at 7 p.m. and sitting down in front of the television. But "this heart was bold ... it never embraced cowardice."

He was quite aware of the million-fold hostility surrounding him. To register the others' resistance, he had merely to change the channel to CNN or BBC World. Really, he didn't have the time for that. Or the inclination. Of the hundred days by which his presidency would be measured, 21 were already spent, and the world remained unchanged.

He hadn't envisioned anything. Hadn't even reckoned on actually making it into the White House, on the world awaiting his decisions. At the same time, he needed to rest, channel-surf, sleep peacefully, wake up and refuel through his contact with the others. There was always a group standing or walking around him, firing him up. That left only three or four hours in the middle of the day in which he was fully active and capable of dealing with business.

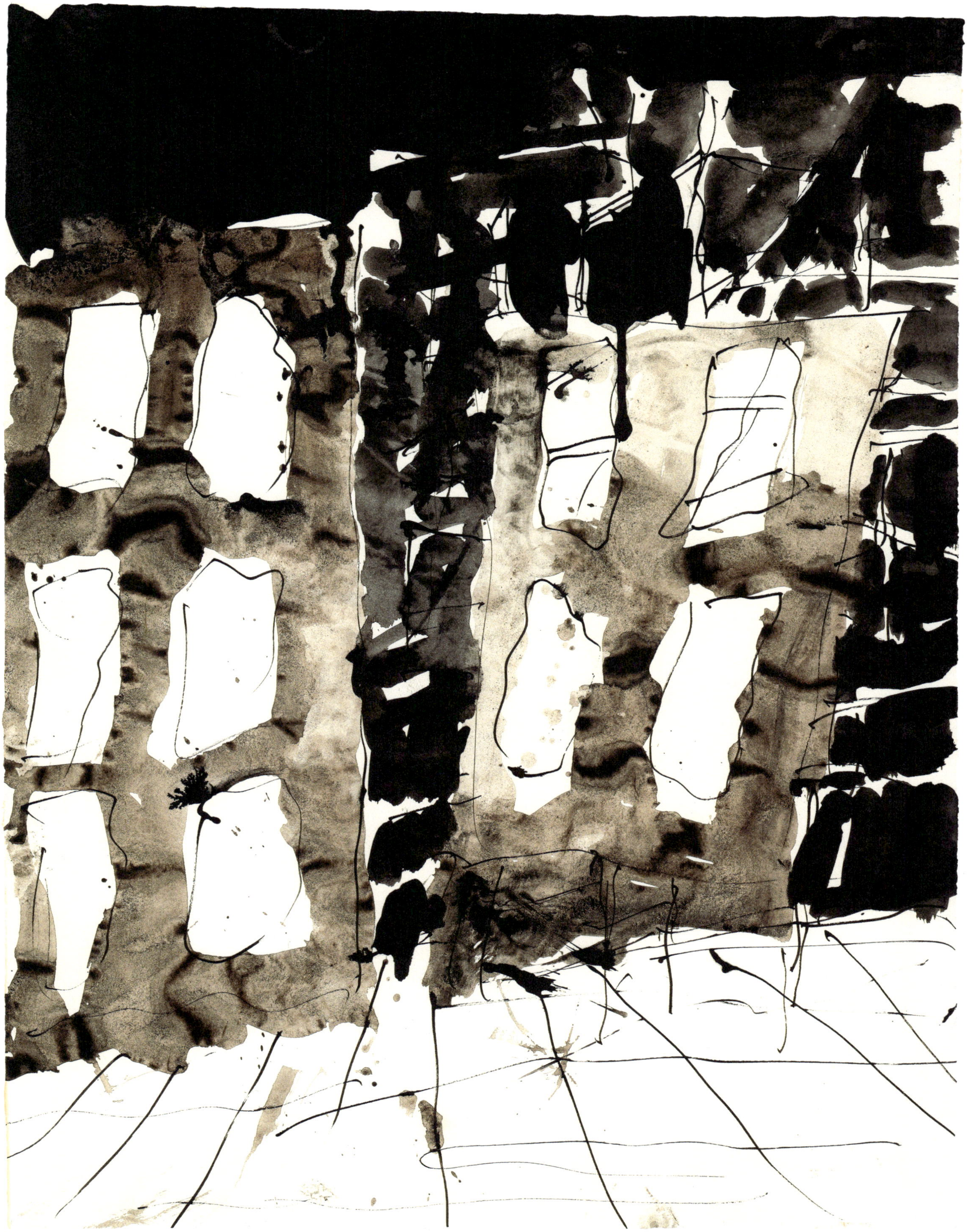

2017

Set design, rejected

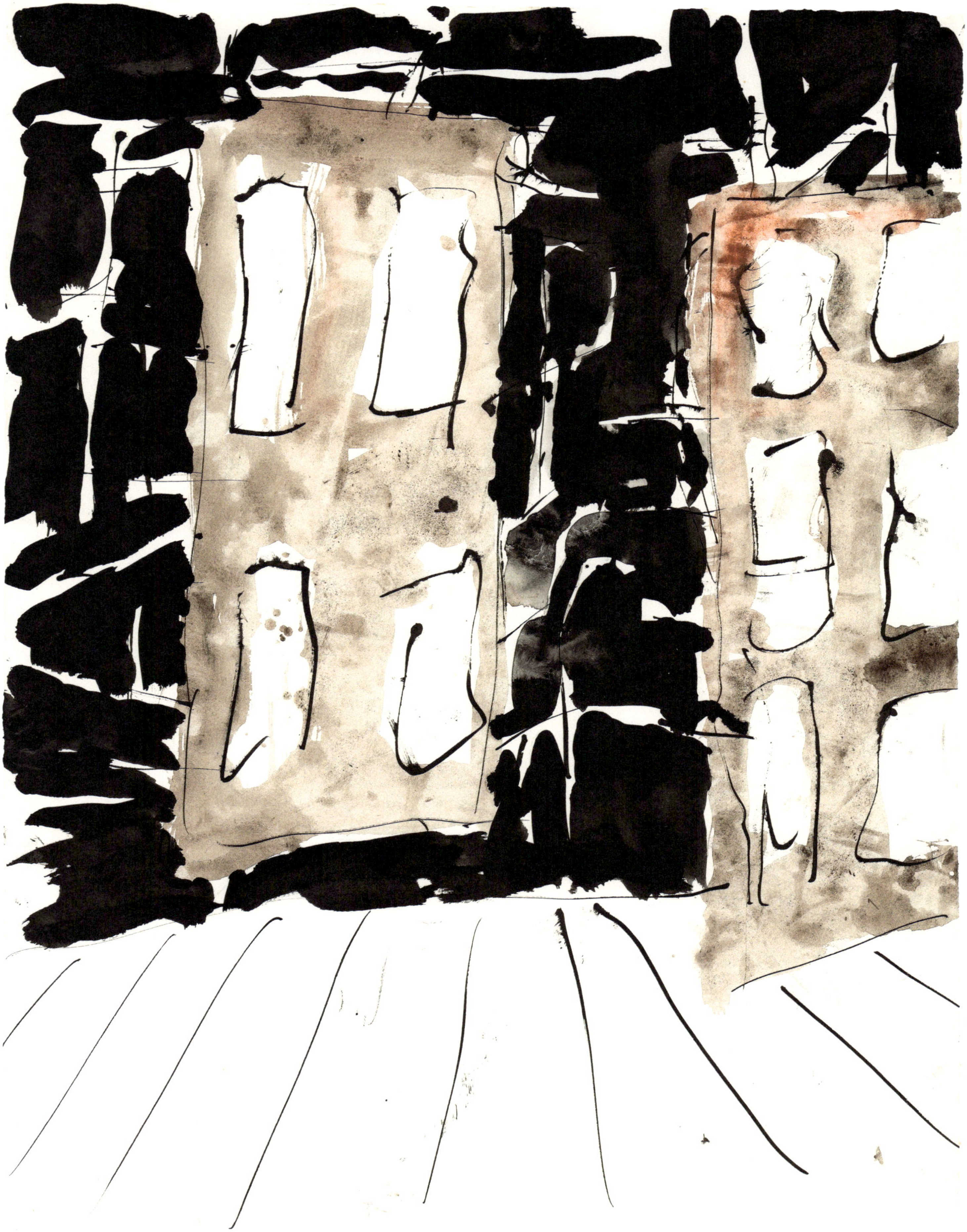

2017

Set design, rejected

“WHEN DOUBTS MOVE THE HEART, THE SOUL TURNS SOUR”

Donald Trump had built up a spiritual resistance against doubts much as others drink lemon juice every morning to keep colds at bay. Doubts never did plague him. Where in the White House (perhaps in the cellars?) was that secret juice that stirred up the world? Much searching, no finding. And that little suitcase that could unlock Armageddon proved—so the president was told when it was handed over to him—not to be omnipotent. Unless the military administration obeyed the coded command, no results could be obtained. In questions of life nothing functions as a machine. The magpie is a thieving, greedy bird. As described by the poet, its feathers are black and white. So, too, the signature under the decrees is bluish black on a white paper background. That clouds the witnesses’ judgment.

“For the foolish it goes much too quick,
They fail to grasp the lesson’s sense”

We pass judgment on God’s will, which brought us this president’s astonishing electoral victory, as though the results of current history depended on his intentions and qualities. But perhaps God just means to use his toxicity to inoculate the world?

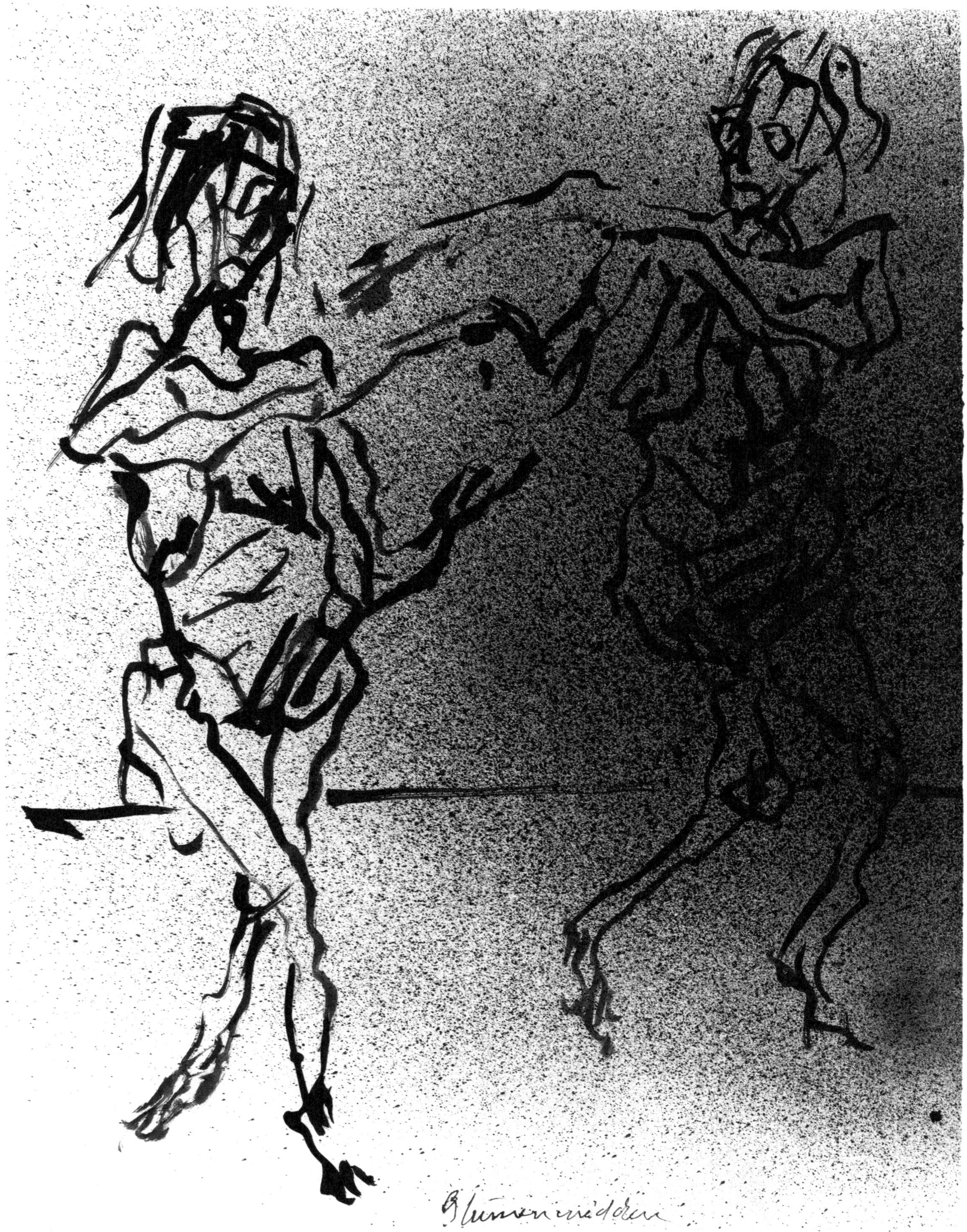

2017 Flower girl

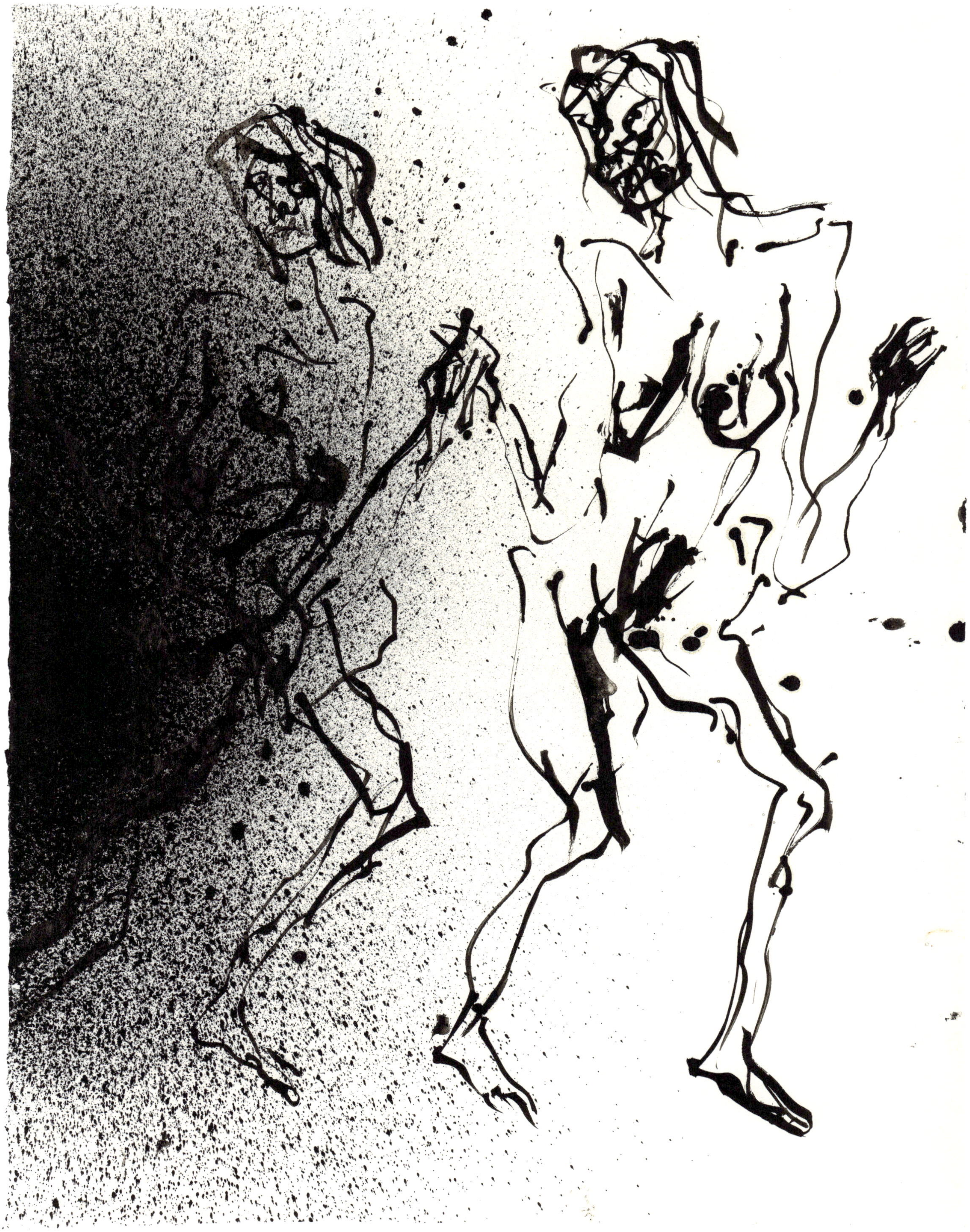

2017 Flower girl

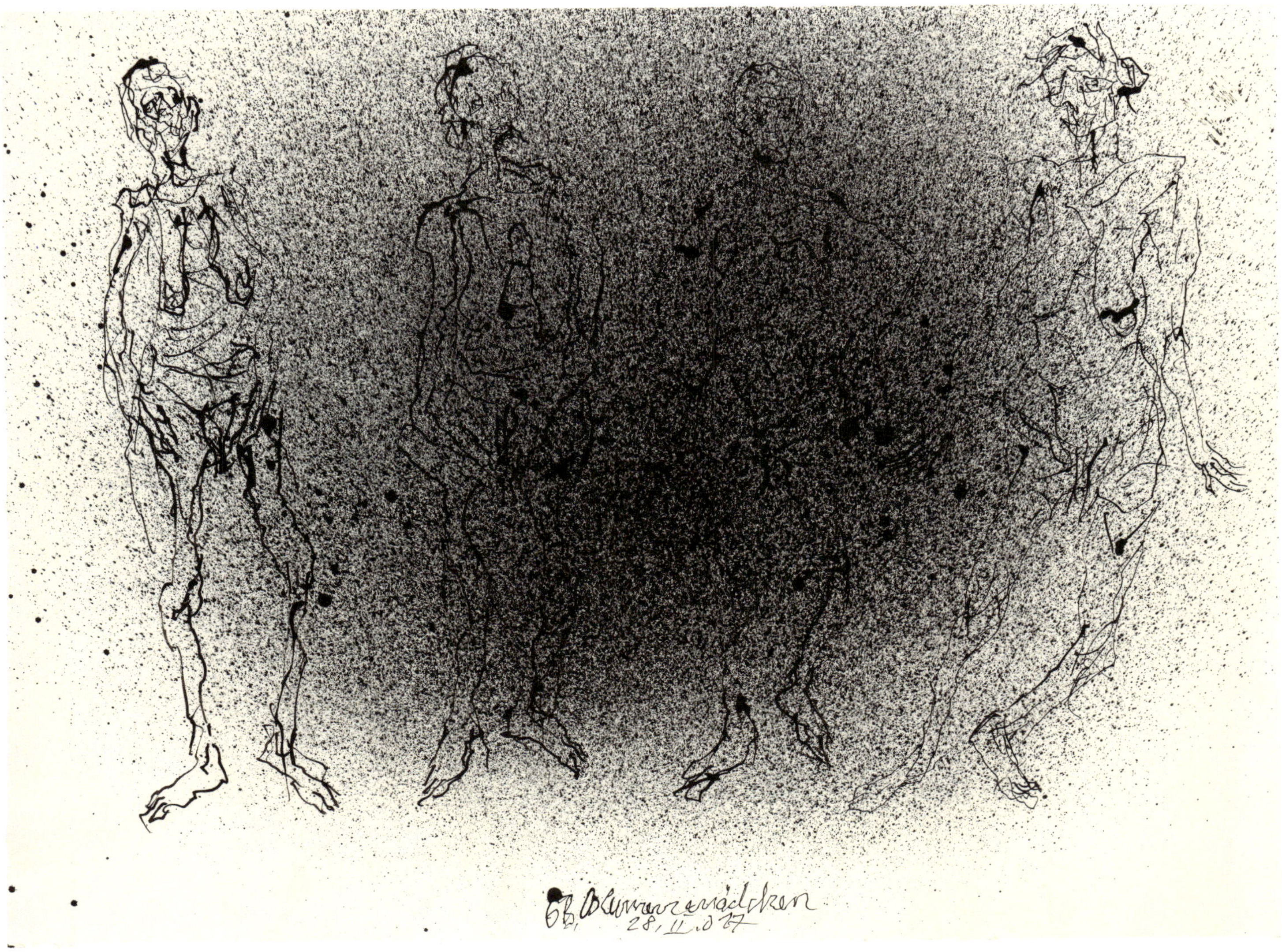

Flower girl 2017

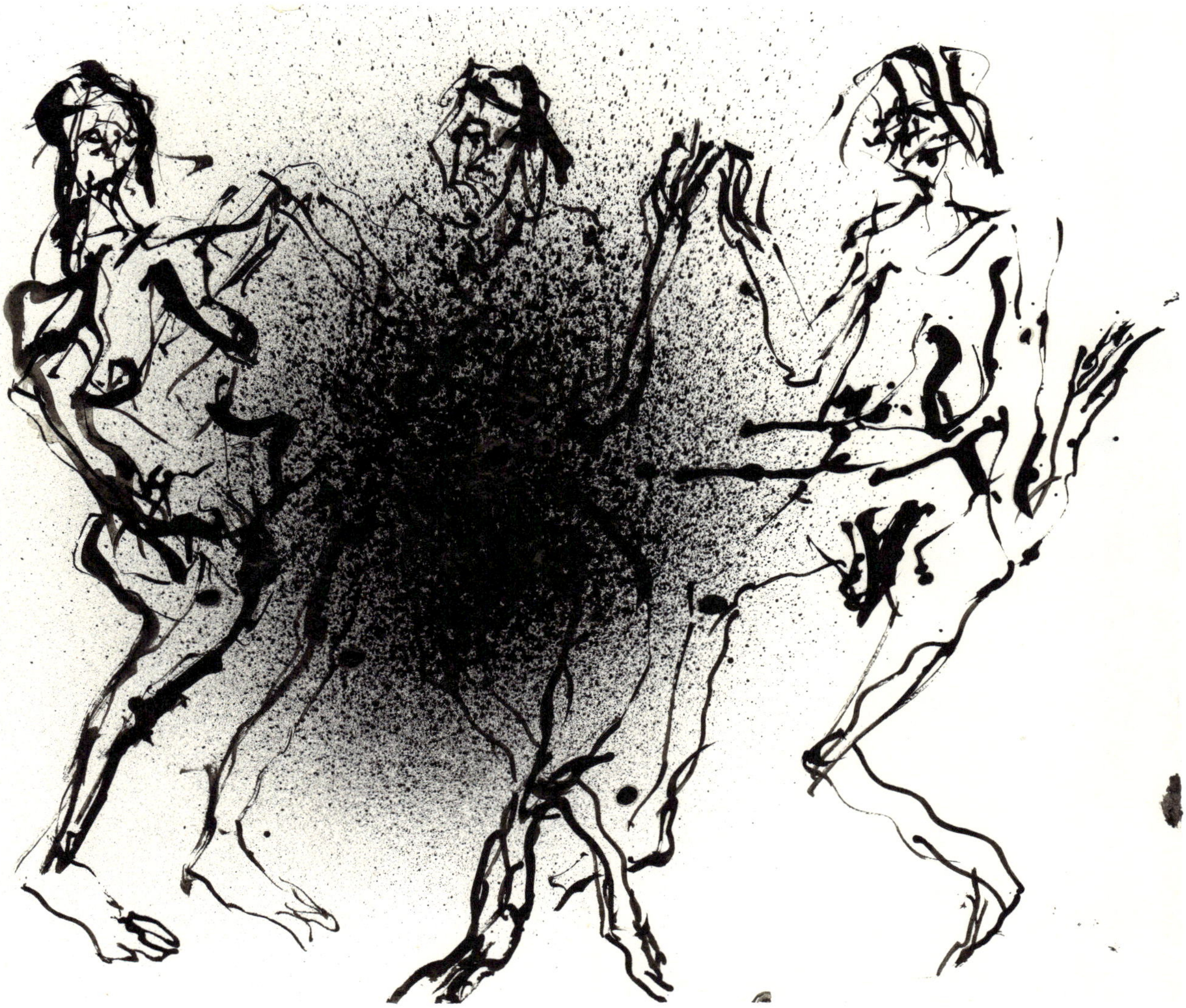

2017 Flower girl

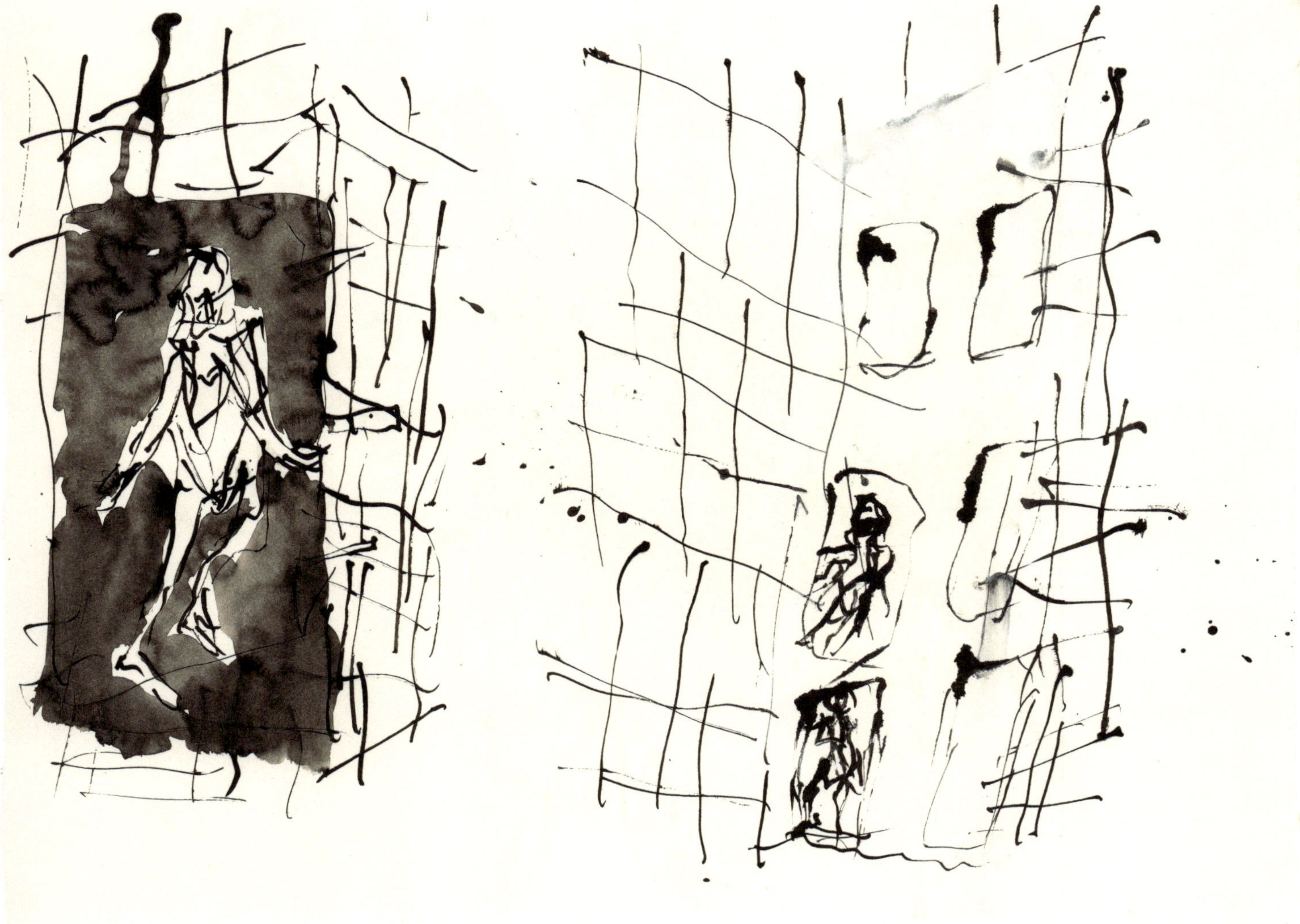

Set design, rejected

2017

THAT CHAMELEON, DEMOCRACY

Democracy, a gigantic beast with striped skin, not black and white, but grey-purple, beige-pewter, shoe-polish-rusty like a discolored zebra, has a surprising way of turning its wishes into reality. Every 80 years it fundamentally changes direction. It may not always know what it's doing, but in retrospect the outcome always accords with one of its BETTER WISHES.
And so, in January 2017, "Unleashed Drama" moved into the White House.

STRONG DISRUPTION!

I was washed into the White House by the wave of new appointments. I'm responsible for putting together the BUDGET IN A HURRY. We have just two weeks to negotiate this NOVEL IN NUMBERS in Congress and with the institutions. All I know is the bookkeeping of my parent company, an oil firm.
I don't know any foreign countries, I know nothing of the existing contracts, haven't acquainted myself with the programs and positions over which the budget now sweeps like a weather disaster. I negotiate, record results, check the page numbers. Certain things disappear from the figures of previous years, certain other things slip in. Evolution rarely has any observers. Nor, in a strict sense, do I "observe," for I know nothing of the things I have at my disposal.

In the days following January 20, Inauguration Day, the president wore his two fool's costumes underneath his armor: that of the building contractor and the TV host. When he swapped the armor of his office for pajamas in the evening, the fool's costumes (as though part of his innards) stayed next to his skin.

One Friday night, March 16, 2017, a similar hocus-pocus rearranged the place cards on the White House table (set for the next day). That was how Germany's chancellor ended up sitting in the White House kitchen. Out of earshot and reach of the president. The situation was as foolish as could be. It was resolved in minutes by the president's daughter. With an alert gaze, this young witness of history sits straight across from her knightly Sire at the table. She is someone he listens to.

As a building contractor by trade, the man noted the White House's construction flaws and tight quarters right after moving in. Since then he's had remodeling plans in reserve. A huge annex off to the right from the Rose Garden. And a tower over the roof with thousands of square feet of usable floor space. Also, a connecting tunnel to the border wall. The additions to the White House will last longer than his presidency, indeed longer than his life.

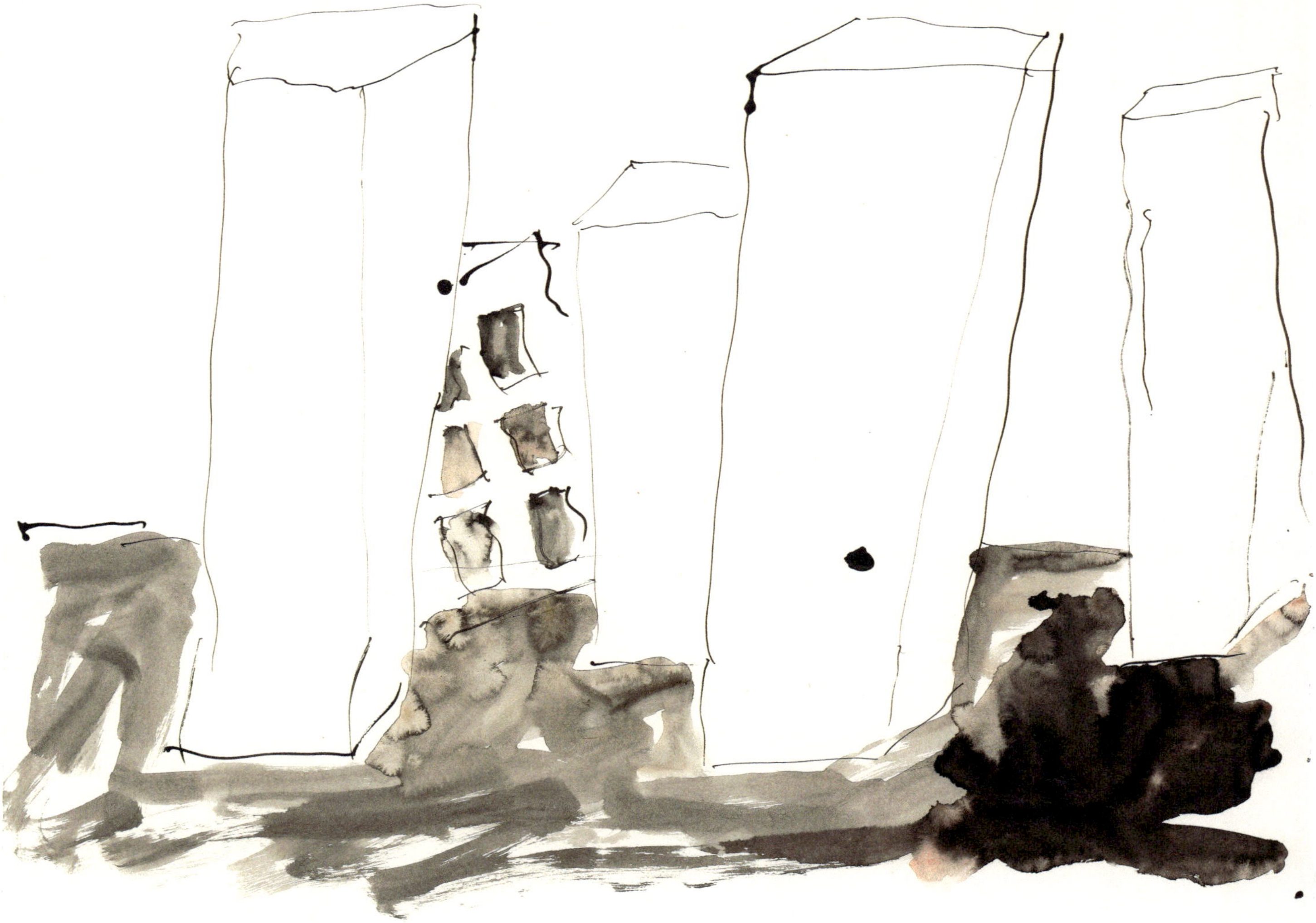

2017

Set design, rejected

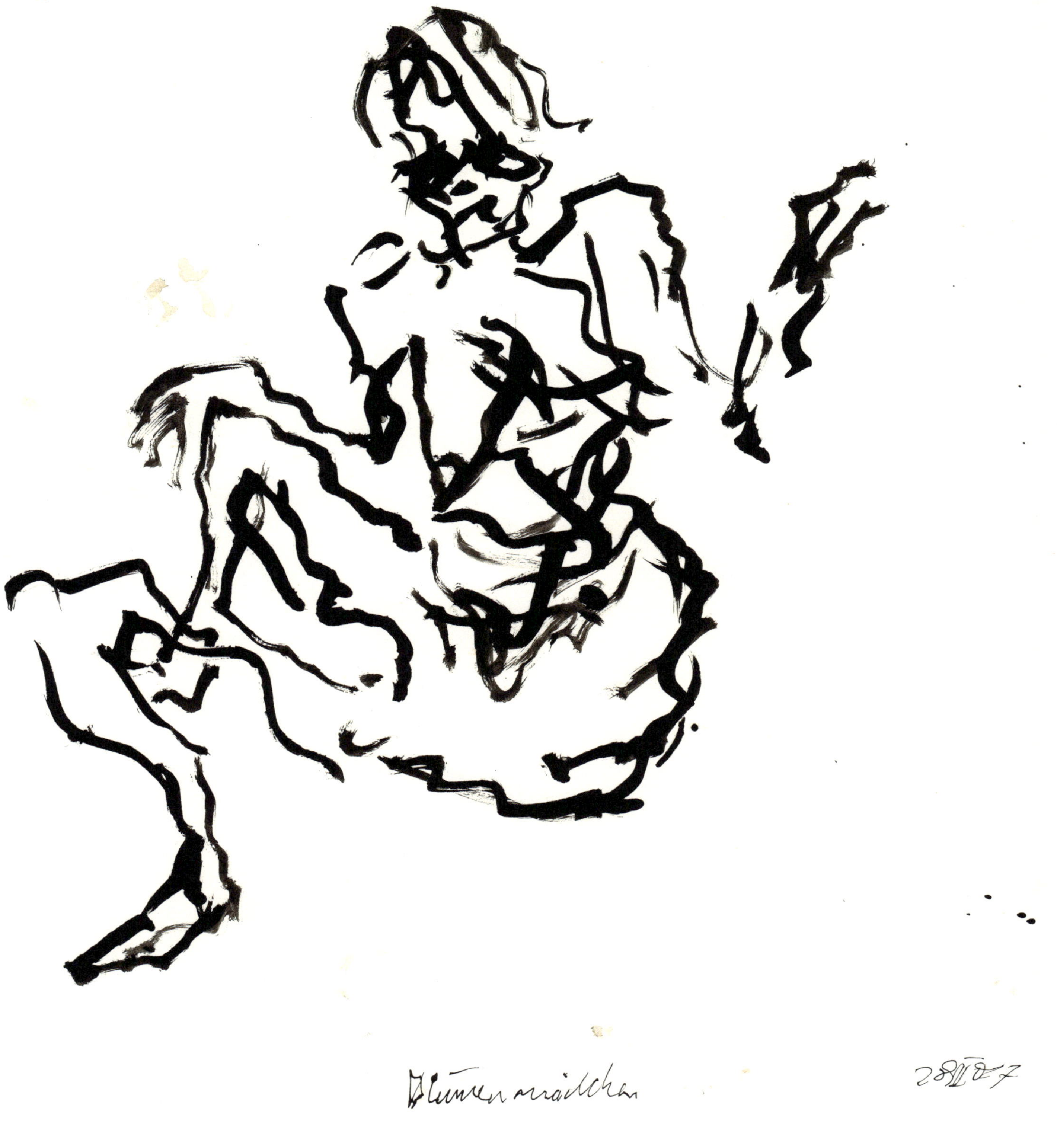

2017 Flower girl

After dinner at the Baselitz family's sumptuous residence and studio we move on to a café. Two wives, two husbands. We switch to straight liquor. I've been sworn to secrecy. At least until the premiere of the *Parsifal* planned for the coming year by the Bayerische Staatsoper in Munich. The subject at hand is the flower girls. What sort of strange creatures are these?

The artistic director of the Bayerische Staatsoper has persuaded Georg Baselitz to create the set design and costume sketches for the Wagner opera. Parsifal is arguably Wagner's most serious opera, says Baselitz, so he can't imagine the flower girls as ornaments or blossoms. He feels that they're "fragments of Herzeloyde." "As if they were part of her." Parsifal feels sorry about riding off and watching as his mother swooned. He didn't go back, didn't turn around his "steed," the donkey he was given. He rode on, and now he yearns for his mother, wondering and wondering—when she fell, was she swooning, or dead? Now everyone becomes his mother: Kundry, the flower girls. In the end, I interject, Parsifal metamorphoses into a powerful woman-soul. Baselitz likes that. There's nothing playful about it. He insists on the phrase "the serious situation that is opera." Herzeloyde is a war widow.

Her husband Gahmuret can't wait nine months for Parsifal to be born. He heads right back into battle. A dead body is all the squires bring back to her. That's something that both Georg Baselitz and I, as children, picked up from our surroundings about the serious situation that is war. The sudden seriousness of the grownups' voices. Women lose their fiancés. A few invalids return. Then, later, the odd prisoner of war. The majority of the prisoners don't return until years later. And the main force doesn't come back at all. So Wagner's flower girls are war widows, Baselitz concludes. That's the reason for the magical music that dominates Klingsor's castle. When we had our dinner and our liquor, Baselitz had not yet designed the womanly bodies of the flower girls, nor the corpulent bodies of the Grail Society's officers.

THE GRAIL'S WARRIORS AND WAR WIDOWS IN THE SKETCHES OF THE PAINTER

As though strung on clotheslines: 36 "emasculated genitals" shown head-down, legs like hooks. Every midnight they step out of their suspension and sit down at the table, rehearsing the hope that a redeemer will come. What costume do the war widows wear? They go naked. Real fates are at stake; you can't stick a person in any old costume. "Just now on proud steeds, now they're shot and they bleed." One of the war widows from 1943 (historic) has preserved in her underthings the scent of the man she loved. Invisible. Three days later (the length of his trip to the front) word of his death arrives.

THE TERM "FLOWER GIRLS" AS CONFUSED WITH A SYMBOL OF HAPPINESS

26 very young women connected with Infantry Regiment No. 12 (each, after her man and spark of hope had died on the battlefield, had turned to another woman who likewise had lost her beloved, none of them feeling able to survive on their own) agreed to share the only two returnees from the disaster at Stalingrad, both of whom, maimed, had been flown out from the front. War, the butcher, had spoiled the two officers' bodies (and their souls as well). And so a community formed around these two "leftover men." A fire lit by female solidarity. The group made parachute silk for the Luftwaffe. Then two of the women got pregnant. The group was not recognized by any religious congregation. They called themselves "flower girls." Due to a confusion; they thought the term came from the flowers that would have been scattered at their weddings, if they'd had weddings. They wanted to see those flowers replaced by a symbol invoking happiness, not death.

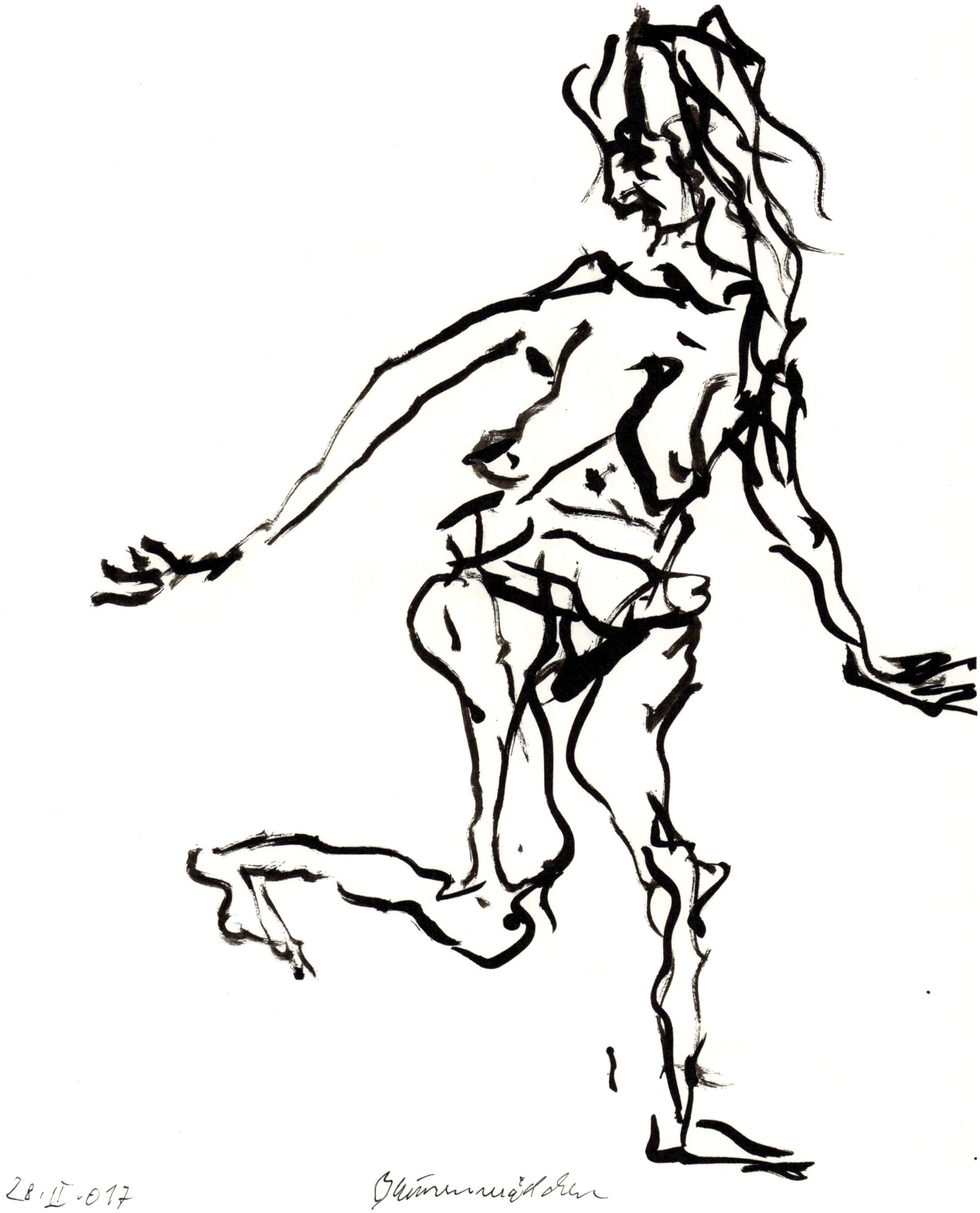

2017 Flower girl

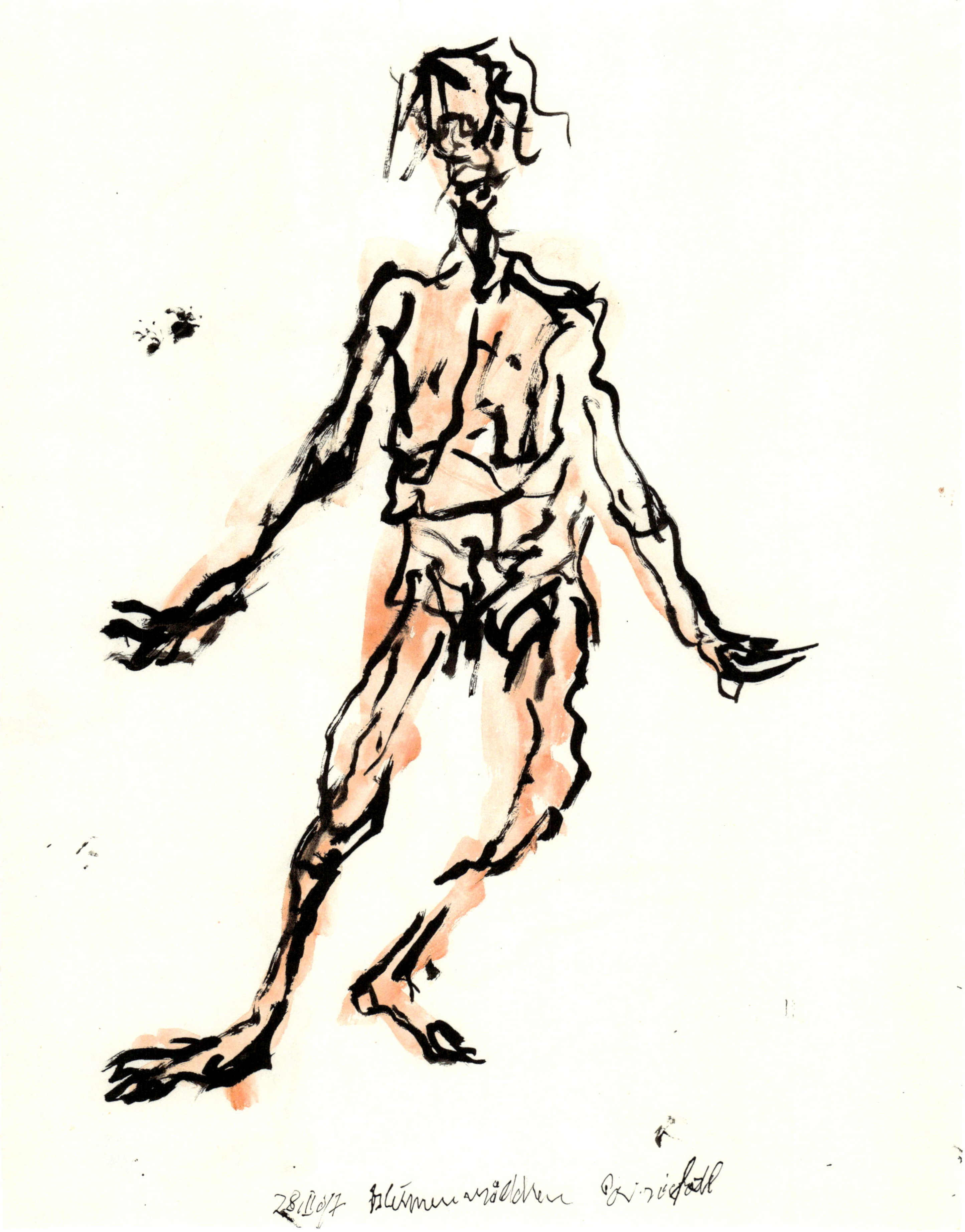

Flower girl Parsifal

2017

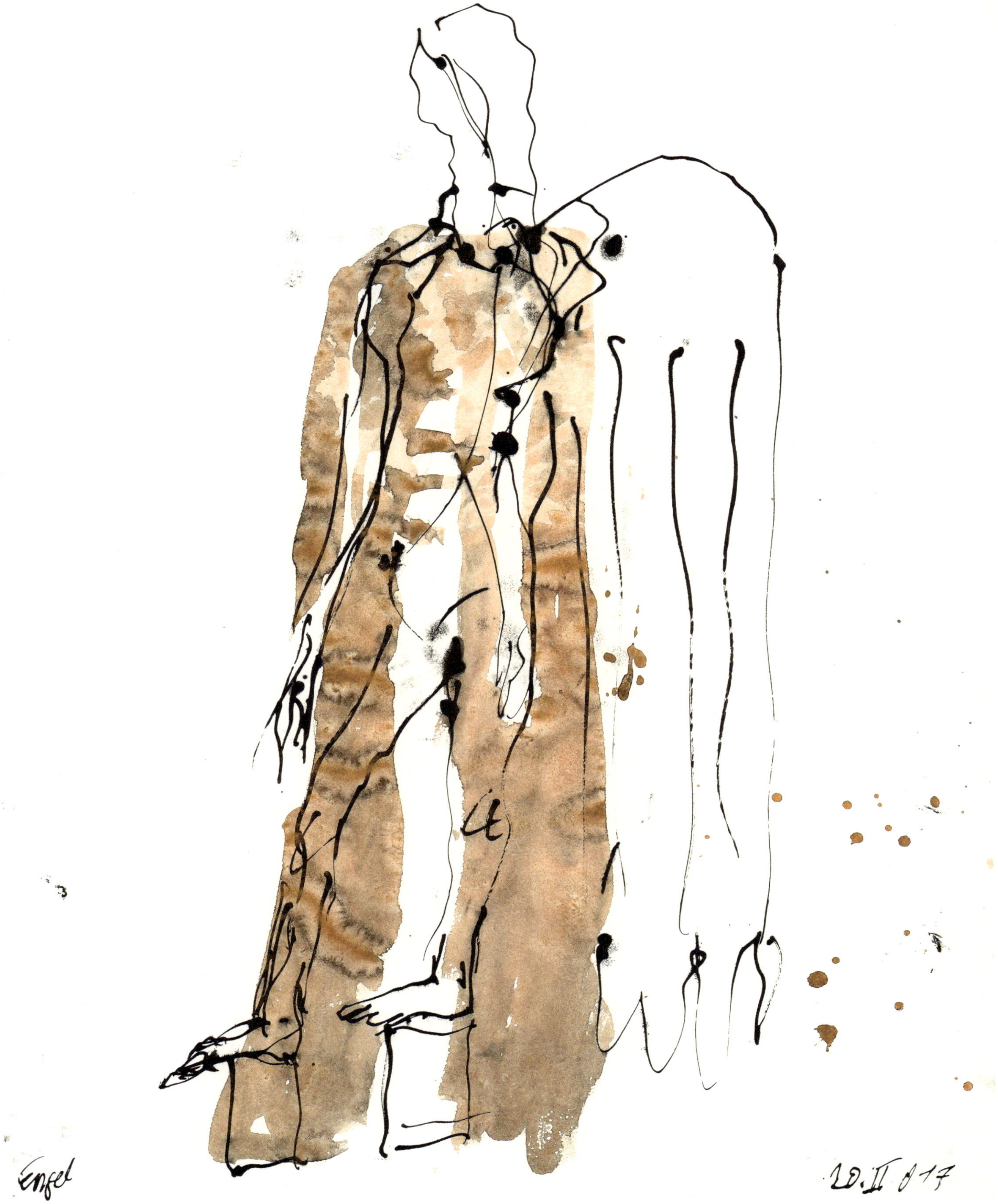

2017 Angel

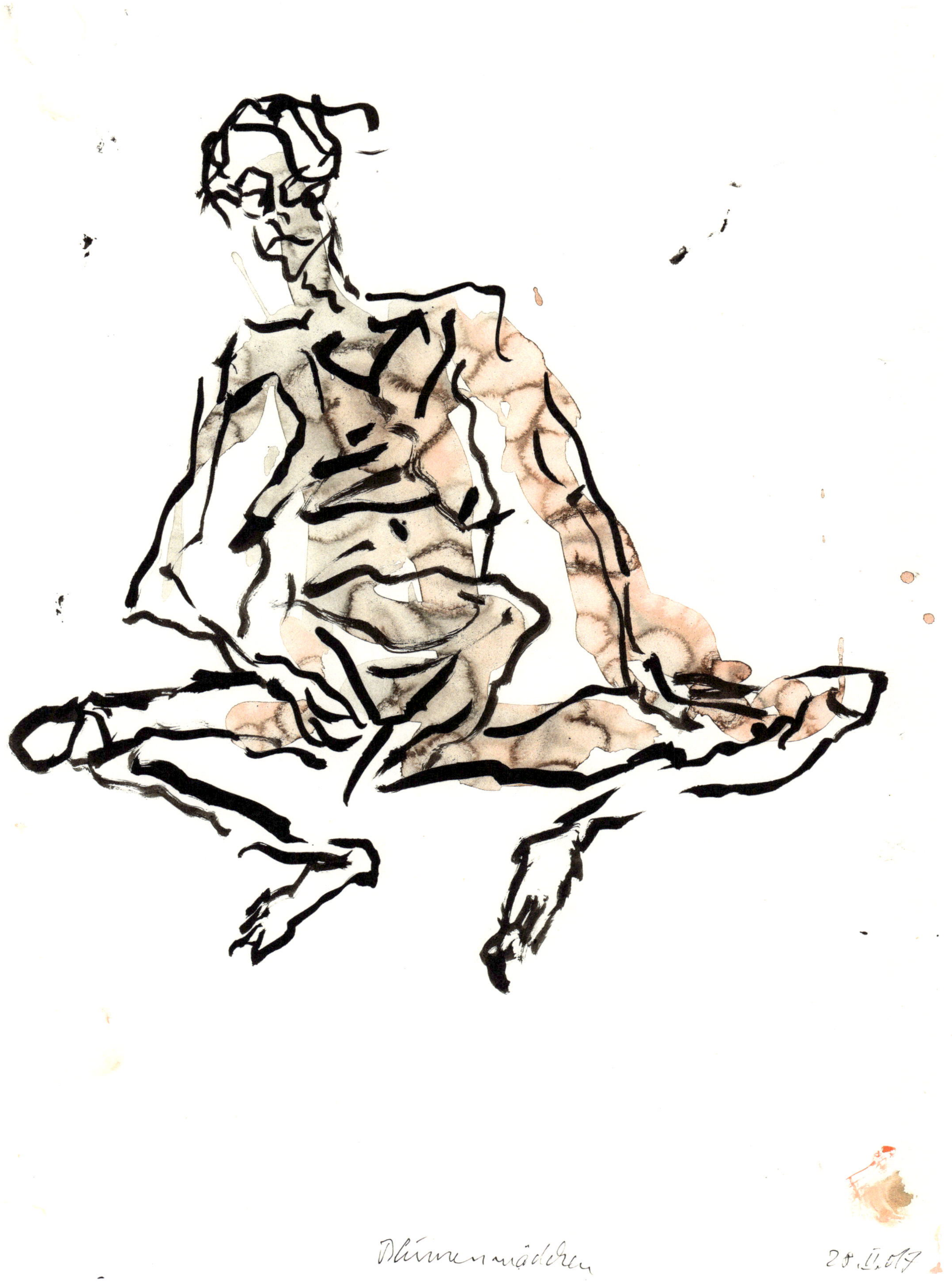

2017 Flower girl

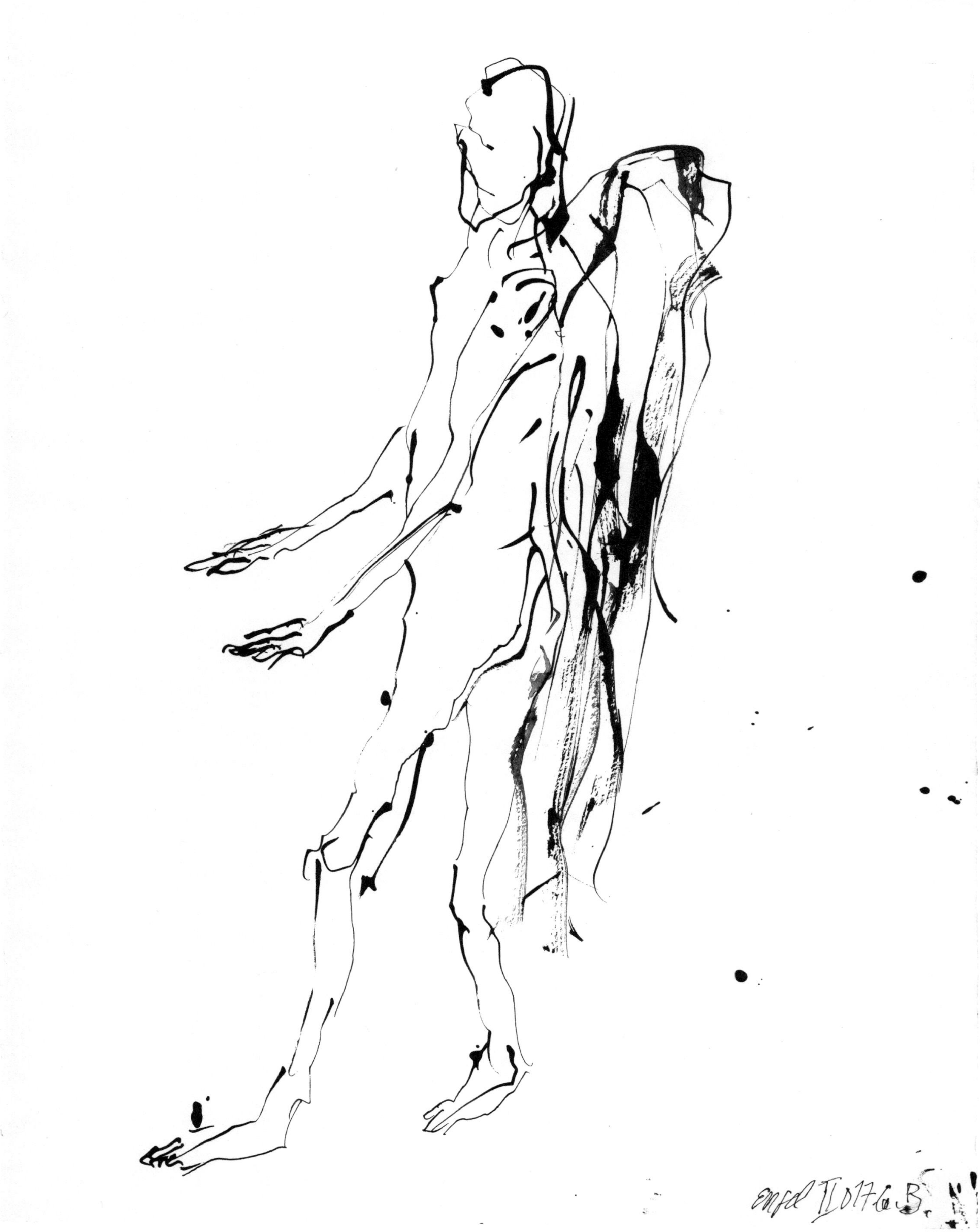

Angel 2017

"TWO LANCE-MEN FROM THAT TILTING TRIBE FAMED FAR AND WIDE FOR MANY JOUSTS"

Two high-ranking US generals, specialists for military reform, proponents of digitally networking the forces, were tripped up by their relationship with a subordinate officer. Each of the two had, for a time, enjoyed that scheming woman's favors. As officers and gentlemen, they'd exchanged e-mails regarding the matter. Military intelligence "decoded" the tangled correspondence between the parties concerned. Without any sensitivity toward the emotions involved. The "text" pieced together by the analysts diverged sharply from the actual events. It had been put in a sequence that seemed incommensurable with the officer's code of honor, the rules of West Point. And so both heroes were forced to quit the service. Hissed curses in e-mails. A ruthless struggle for a beautiful mistress. This was no knightly contest for a lady. The object of their affections was unable to decide on one or the other. Thus the voluminous correspondence. Awkward: the language of love versus the language of duty. The dismissal of these leading Afghanistan generals knocked out a quarter of America's military strength. Two thirds of its drive for reform. The decision in this duel for the sought-after woman came not from a god, but from the Inspector General of the United States. In charge of investigating officers from general majors on upwards, he answered only to Congress, and ruled that the intelligence services have blanket permission to read the e-mails of all members of the military. The exposure of that tangled game of love: a random outcome.

WHEN THE SENSES DECEIVE, THEY ARE UTTERLY THEMSELVES

Antikonie, a corruption of the name of Sophocles' tragic heroine. A fresh, medieval creature. Long since open to the notion (even before knowing him) of entrusting herself to the hero Gawain. To get acquainted, the two would have had to spend 24 solid hours telling each other their stories. They didn't have that time. They chose trust instead of knowledge. Antikonie's INNER GLASSES covered up her nose as well. She didn't smell Gawain's sweat, nor the stench that rose from the unwashed hero's crotch and anus. Instead, she transformed that scent into something that, if she'd had the words, she would have called the "scent of angels' harps." She was confusing that with "angel hair." *Neurotransmitter*, irregular.

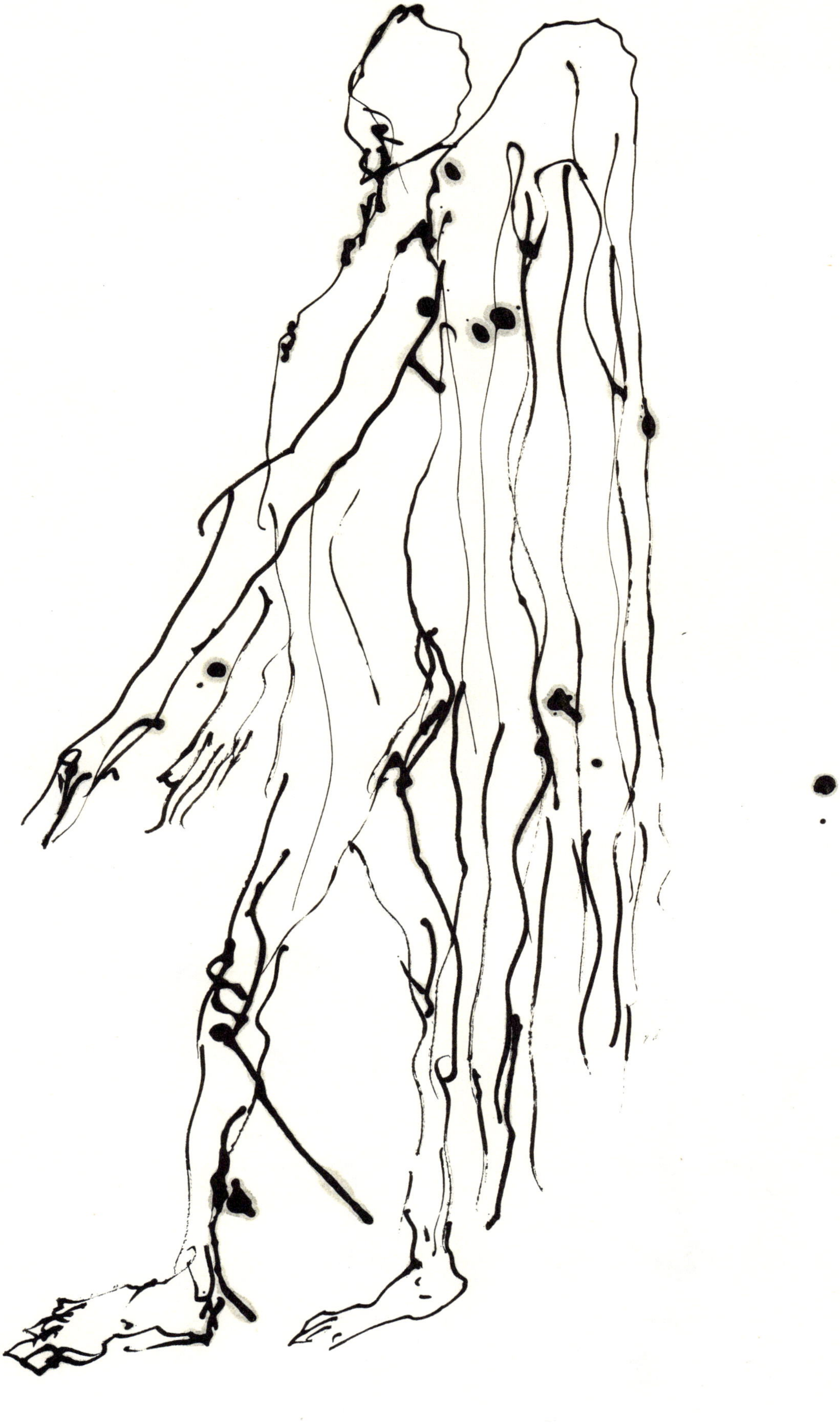

2017 Messenger

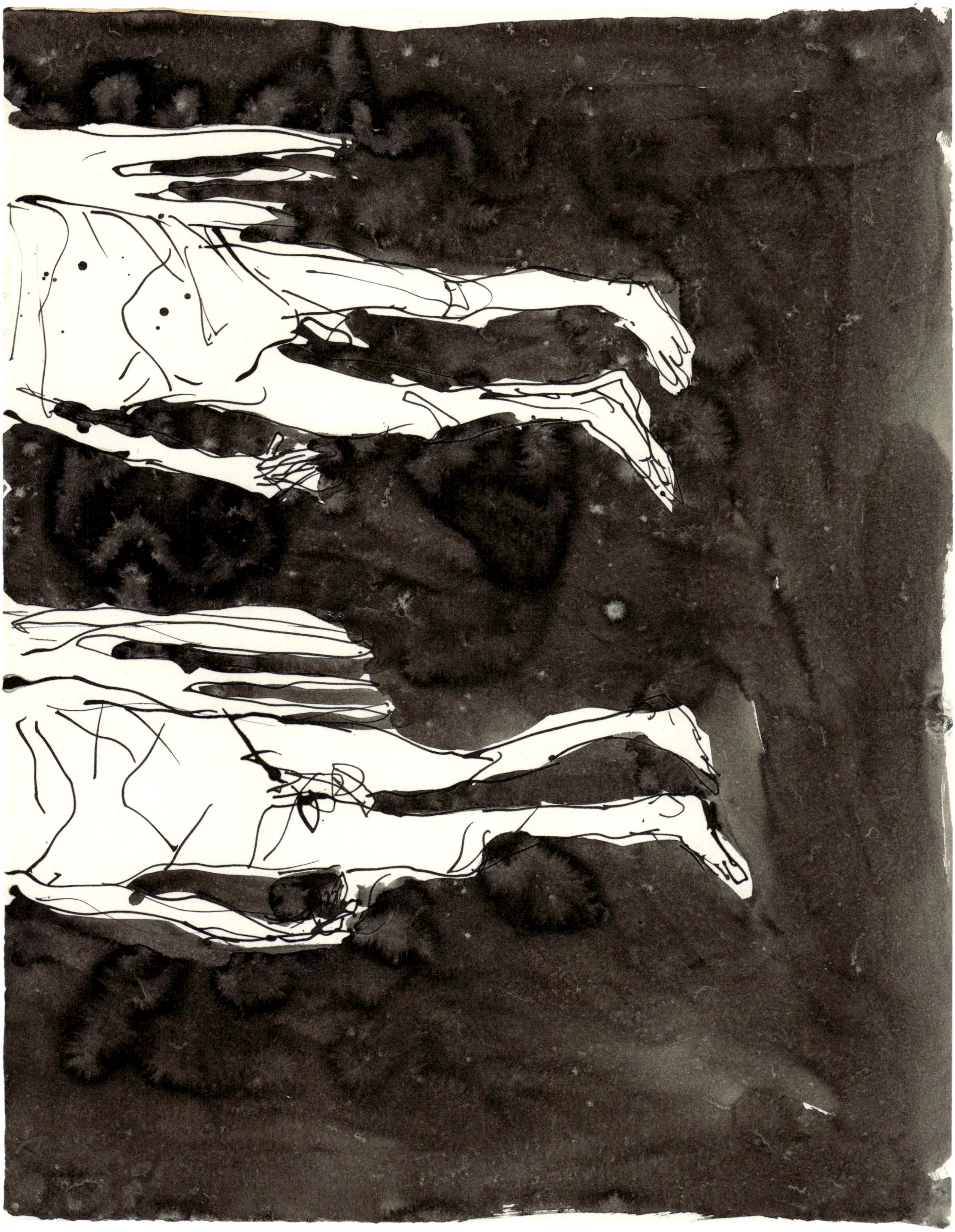

Angels 2016

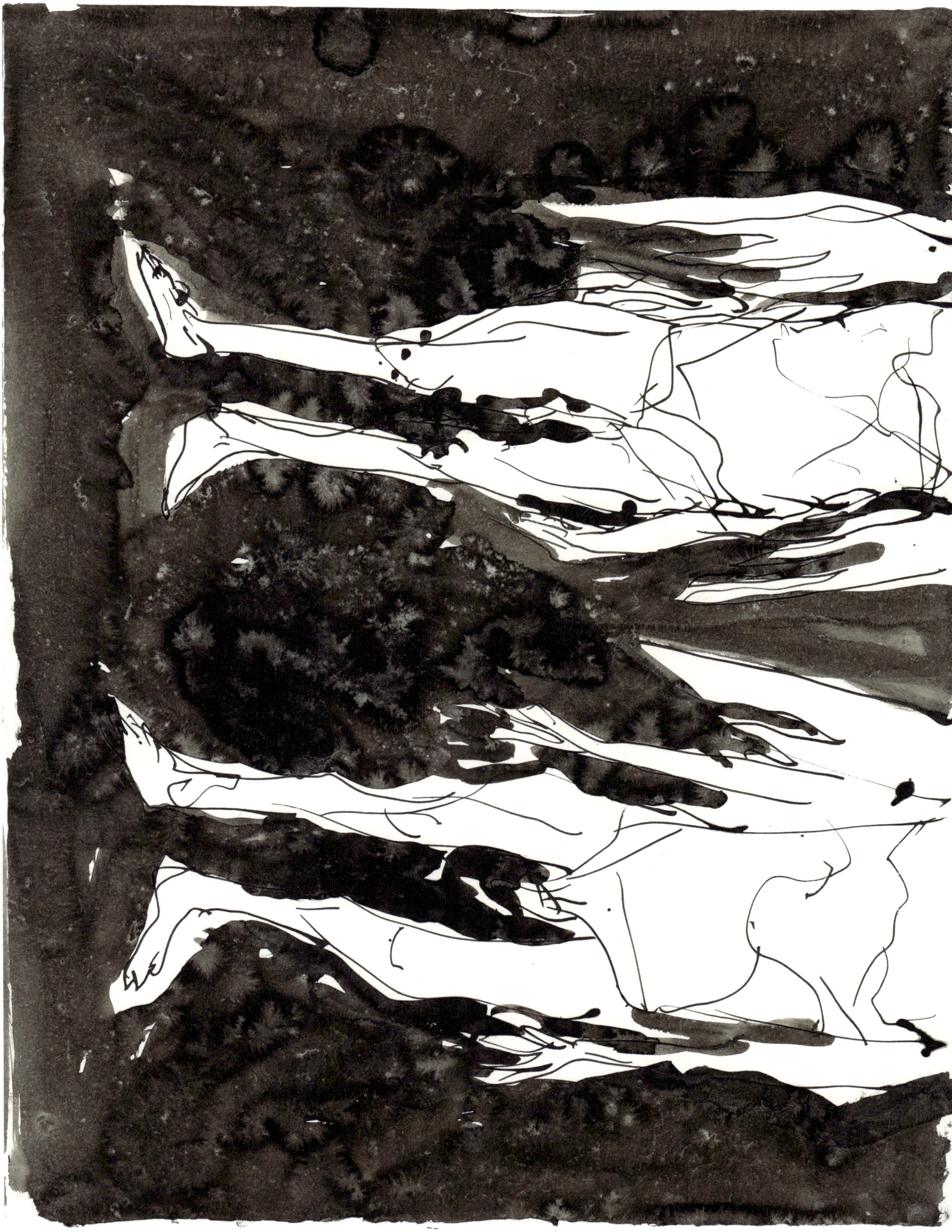

2016 Angels

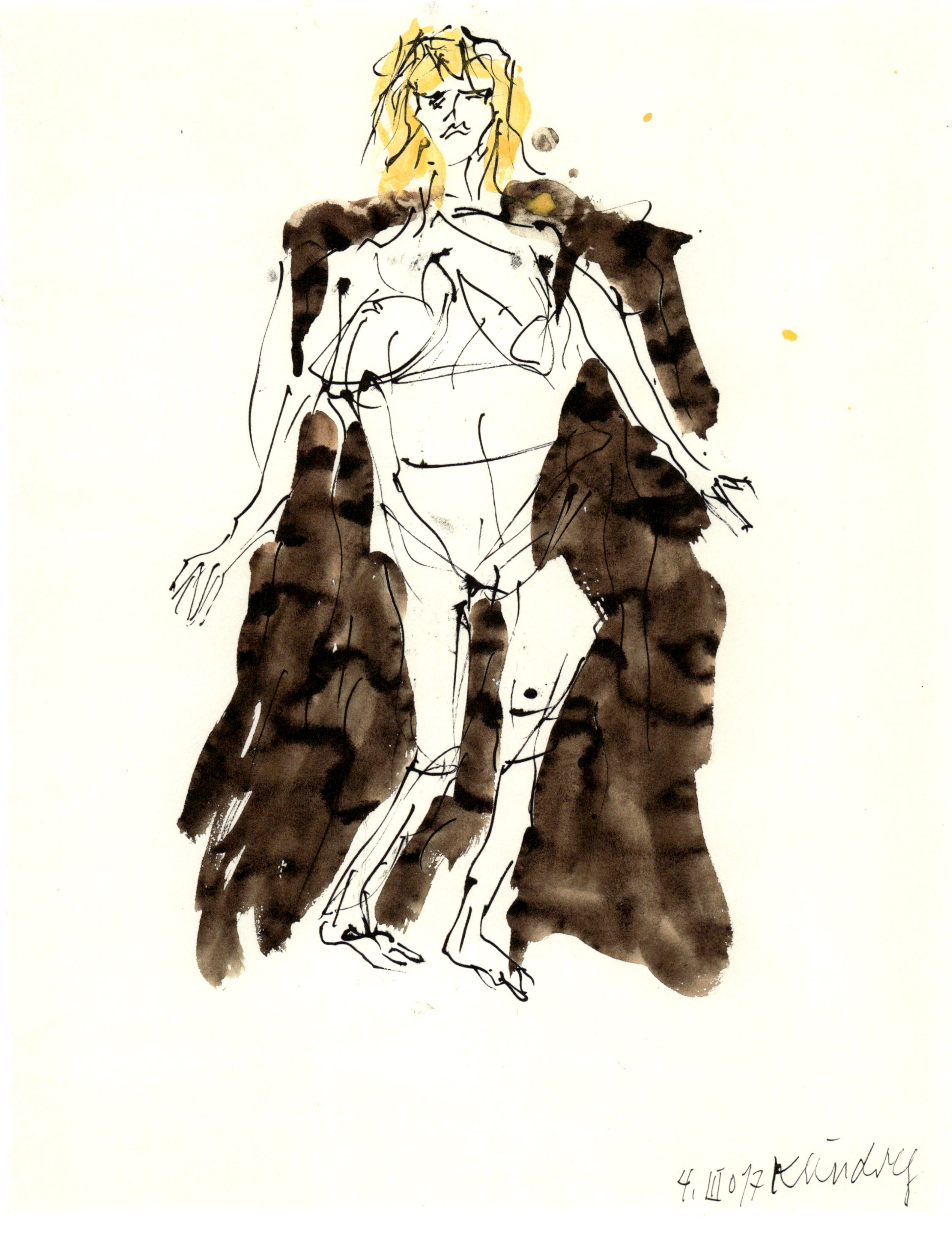

Kundry 2017

3D glasses—through which, as though sitting at a control console, automobile workers can see their work station plus all the options for modifying the work process at hand—interlink reality with activity, which the workers view like blind people. That made me imagine the inner glasses (adrenaline-charged / mystagogic / muscular / nerve-activated / brain-braked / improvisational / necessity-driven) possessed by every person elevated from plowing the fields—that is, every aristocrat.

Antikonie for instance, fresh out of bed, bathed and dressed by her servants, the early sun on her English skin, beheld the bearded Gawain through ardor-glasses that transformed the warrior into the only person Antikonie—so she declared—could ever love. Thus it was decided, anti-hierarchically, in the people's assembly of her body, with all her senses presiding. She couldn't see the knight as he stood before her, weary, spent from two days on horseback; she transformed this WORK STATION OF HER FUTURE LUST INTO AN IDEAL. Her medicine cabinet had various intoxicants at the ready.

“THIS UNBAPTIZED ADONIS FOUGHT FOR WOMEN’S FAVORS”

Feirefiz of Anjou. Born in a far land. The hero Gahmuret, his sire, didn’t wait around for the birth of the child. Had long since returned to the service of the caliph.

The PIEBALD boy, the zebra-striped son of the black queen Belakane and a hero who, when nude, was colored matte pink, must not be pictured as a Mohammedan. Feirefiz names Jupiter as his god and Juno and Diana as his goddesses. He is a Roman.

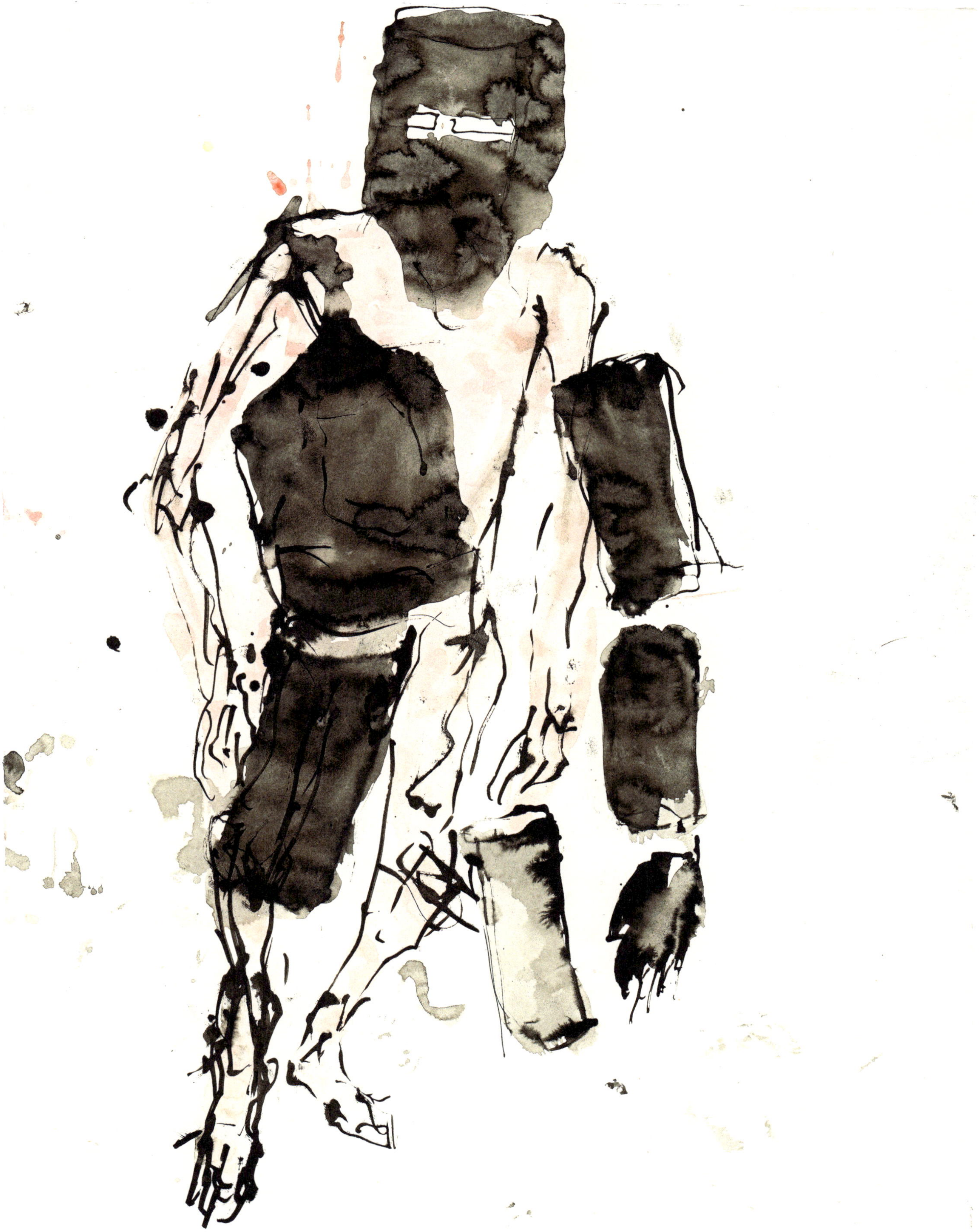

2017 Parsifal

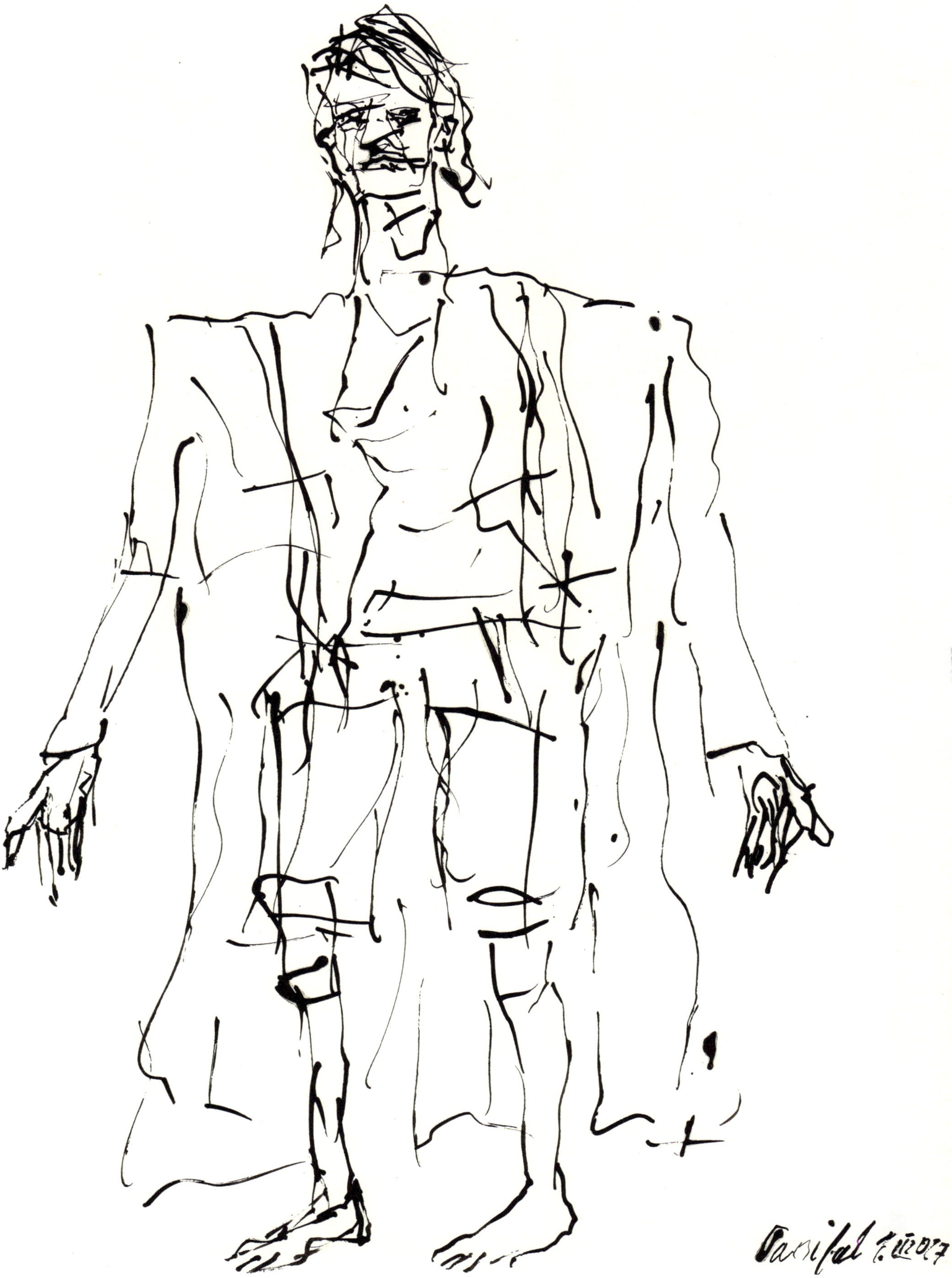

2017 Parsifal

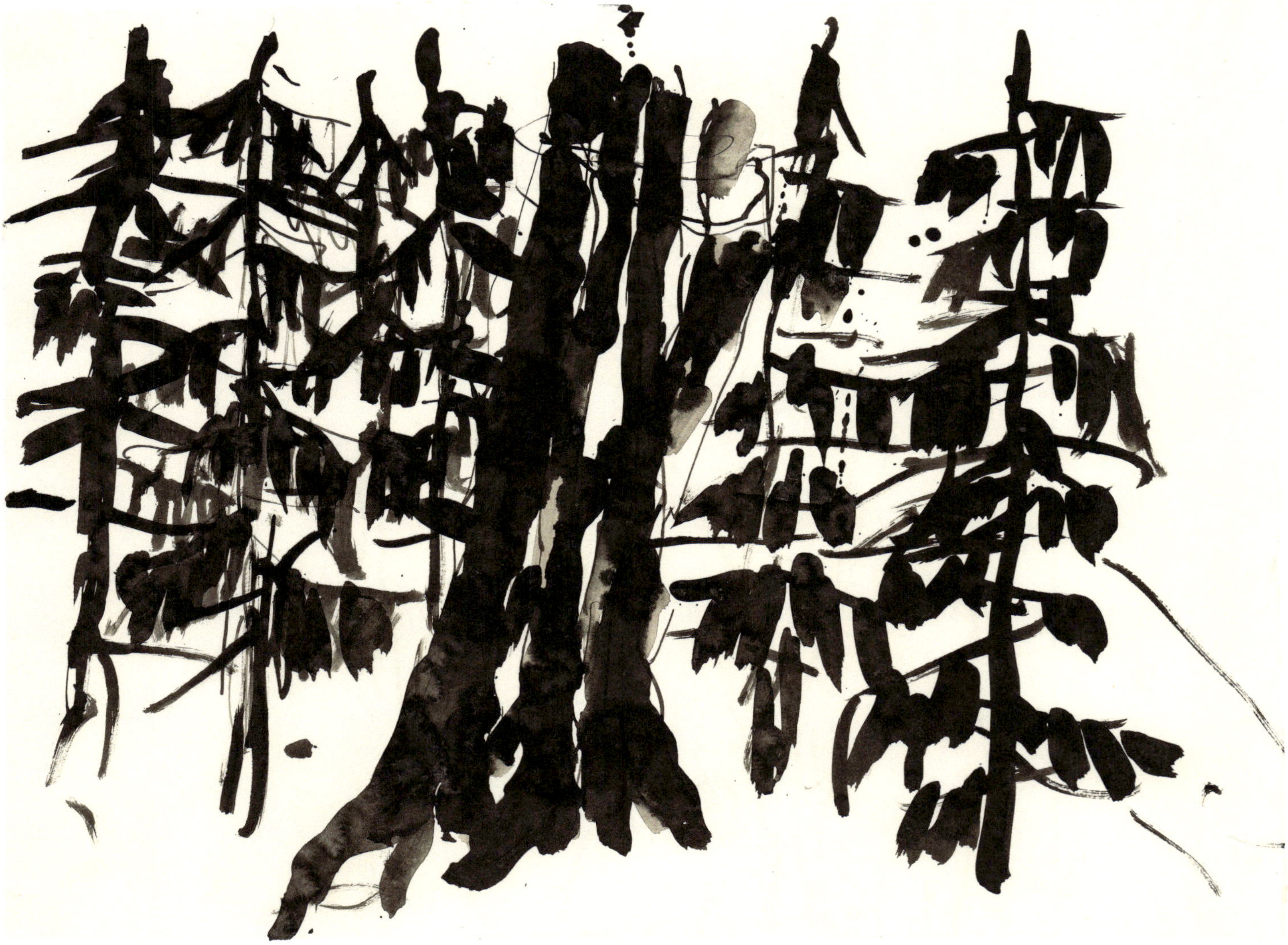

THE BAPTIZED PARSIFAL
has already grown
tired. His movements
have slowed
under the blows of the
HEATHEN, his half-
brother. If no one comes
to his aid, within
minutes he'll succumb.

At that, the iron ones,
the not-yet-born,
Gardais and Lohengrin,
the little ones from the
Land-of-Not-Yet,
snatched him
from his plight with
their strong arms.
Reaching from the future,
they dragged him,
"one already lost,"
into the light
as from a deep well.
His sword was smashed
to pieces.
He could no longer see
quite what was going on.
"Love leads the way!"

WHAT DO PEOPLE DO WHEN THEIR RULERS, BUSY PURSUING ADVENTURES, HAVE NO TIME TO BOTHER WITH THEM?

The great lords of the early Middle Ages sally forth on a whim. That is how adventures come about. Feirefiz (as yet unaware of his half-brother Parsifal) wakes early in the morning in the midst of his army, restless in his own skin. He sets off into the forest. Just to get his muscles moving, the way you loose a pack of dogs.

He'd ridden from his army into the *forêt*
so as to *mouvier* there

Now the "half-brothers without knowing it," Feirefiz and Parsifal, stand face to face. They start by insulting each other and then proceed to do battle. As is the custom for proper knights. Knights in full armor, with their visors down (practically blind), meet for single combat on a marked-off field. They wouldn't keep their armor on at the dinner table. They'd never ride through the woods or down the roads in that get-up. Only in the *Aventiure*, the romanticized narrative, do they meet in full armor, which means that Feirefiz and Parsifal, the half-brothers, wouldn't have been able to recognize each other even if they had known of each other's existence. Each dents the other's armor. As noted: Parsifal loses his sword. And his half-brother, the heathen, in keeping with his splendid upbringing, refrains from killing him. It would bring him no glory to kill an unarmed man. That is the moment in which the As-Yes-Otherworldly, the future sons, rescue their father; they might have failed had it not been for the "benign breach" in Feirefiz' lust for battle.

He offers the unarmed man a truce. They sit side by side in the grass, both rather exhausted. Then, while chatting, they discover that they were half-brothers.

"My father and you, you two and I,
we were utterly one
But we appeared as though divided into three."

The half-brothers are moved. In the morning sun, just a few yards away from them, a labyrinthine forest begins. They're glad that neither of them managed to deal the death blow, though it is what they, as knights, must both aspire to. Feirefiz ascribes this miracle to Jupiter.

"He laughed and he wept—in secret
from his unbaptized eyes."

Under the circumstances, it surprises Parsifal that his half-brother, a ruler, is so generous with his time. On the other side of the woods, so Feirefiz has told him, a whole army is waiting. What do people do when their ruler vanishes from sight, when he has no time to rule them?

Each day, Trump has time for just a fraction of the world that wants to speak to him. If the German chancellor visits him on the 14th of the month, six to nine of the ruler's hours are scattered to the winds. No compensation is found for the cancelled appointments the next day either. His fooleries (stamped signatures under decrees) are swallowed up by big holes in time.

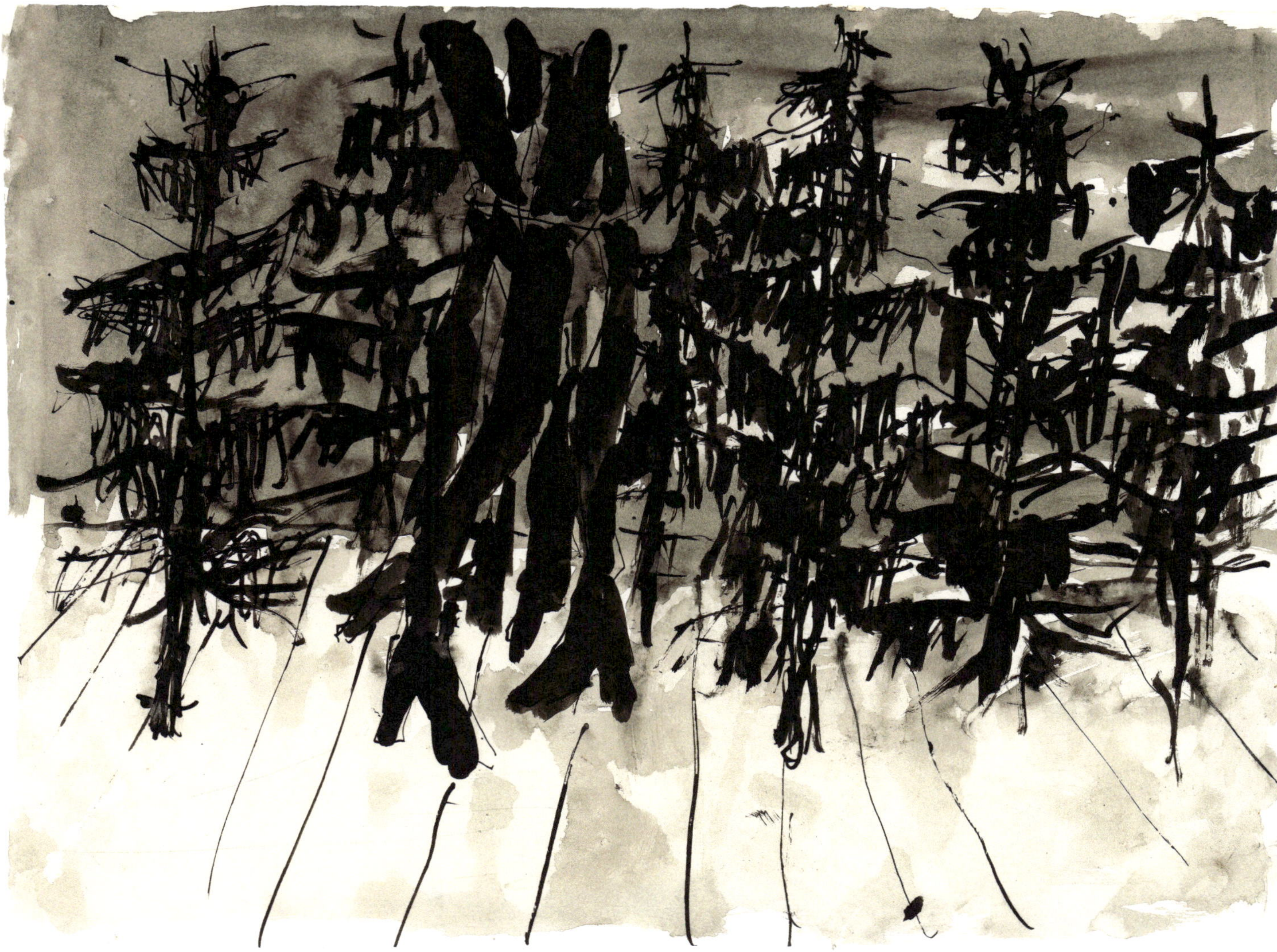

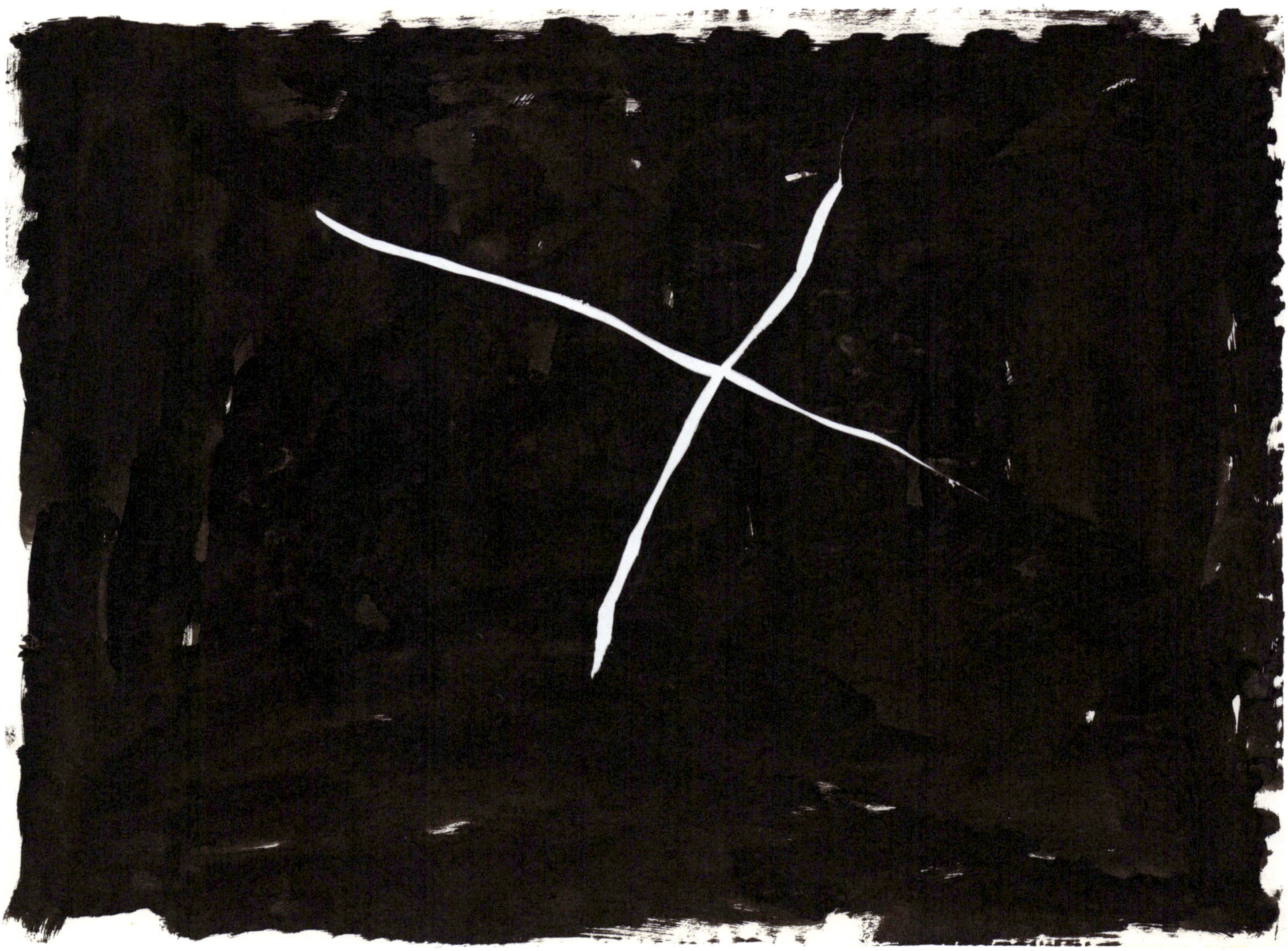

2016

Backdrop, rejected

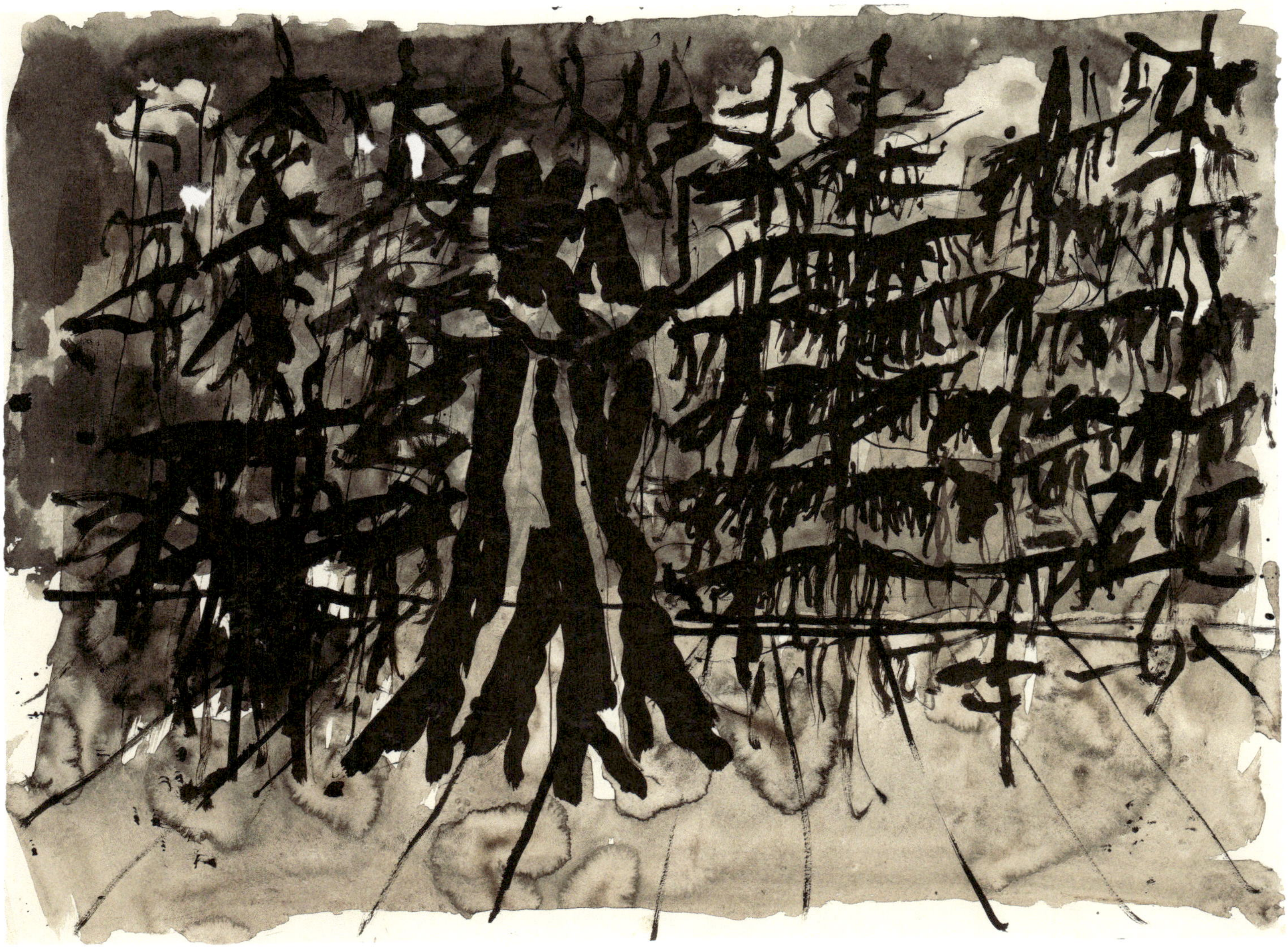

Set design 2017

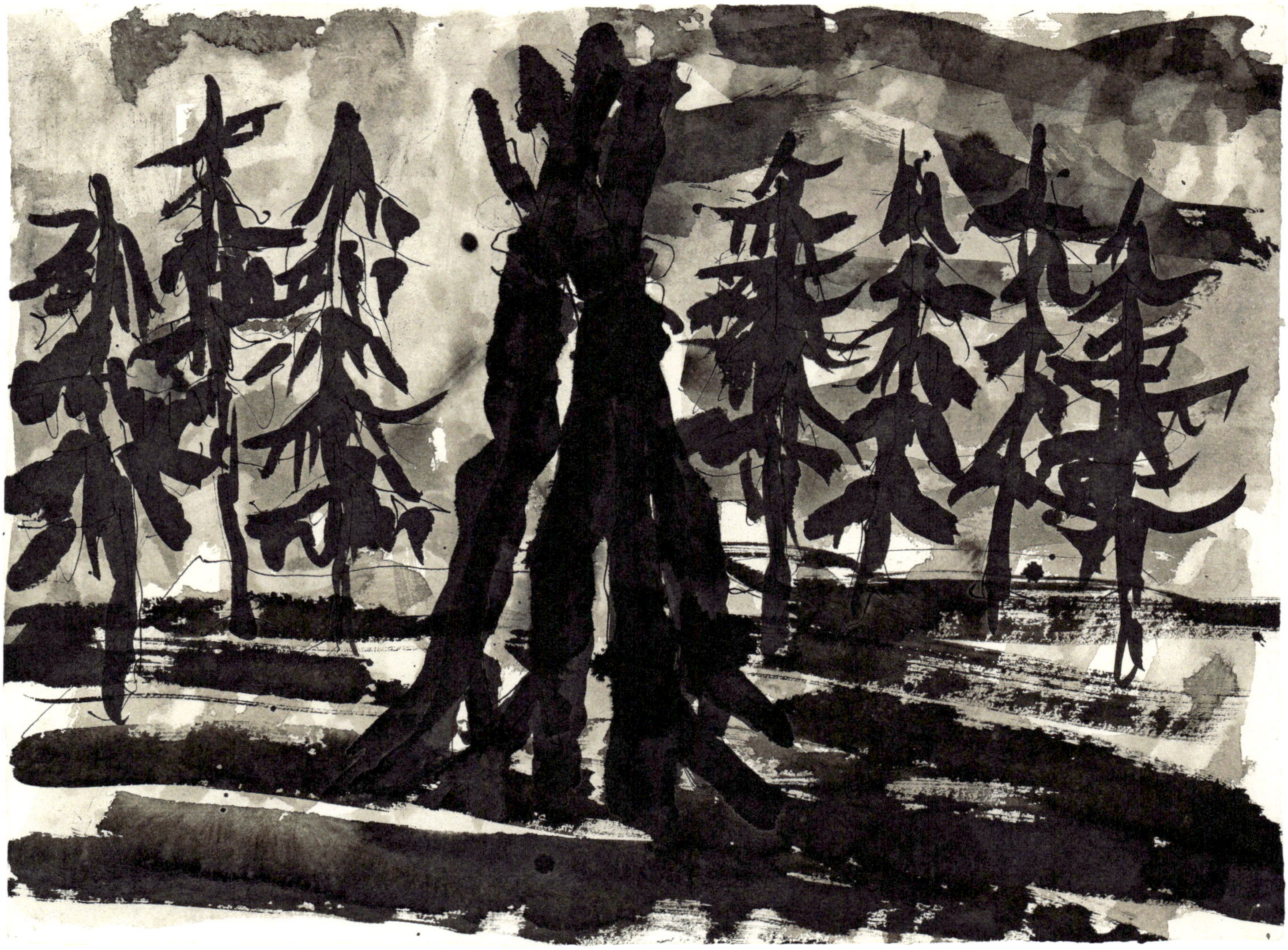

2017

Set design

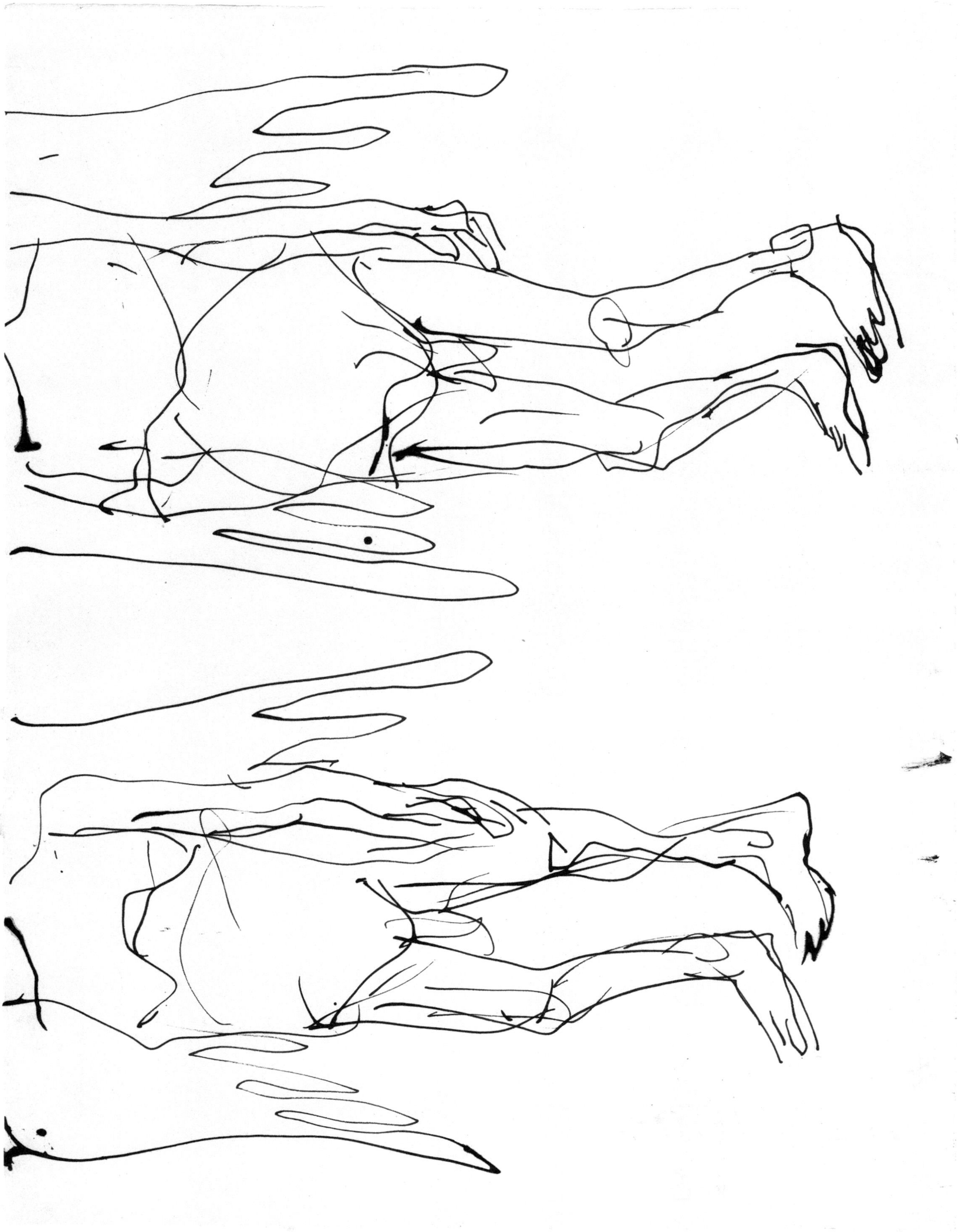

Angels

2017

IN THE YEAR 1000 A.D., THE WORLD NEARLY TURNED SPIRITUAL

In the year 1000 A. D., everyone at the Holy Roman Emperor's court was expecting the LAST JUDGEMENT. Because it was so complicated to travel around his empire, the itinerate emperor Otto III never slept twice in the same place. He expected the Last Judgement to come in November of that year. Military campaigns weren't worth it anymore. No more stockpiling hope. No planning new buildings. The peasants let the harvest rot in the autumn rain. Why fill the barns if winter will never come?

Members of the high nobility arrived and thronged the antechambers of the monasteries. In a CIRCLE OF BROTHERS they planned to await the day of salvation. They planned to obstruct potential damnation with a dam of collective prayer.

They pictured damnation as a sort of mudslide, a surge of wet earth. As the crucial weeks slipped by, the knights and their bondsmen (everyone had come down with colds) went back to their daily routine. For a few years they'd been weaned of the aggression that went with their rank. The collective experience (based on fantasy) had changed them. Few of these devotees of God had children. But it took the children in the surrounding area an entire generation to return to the PREDATORY LIFE of their original ancestors.

In actual fact, the Chateau Mont Mirail, whose underground caverns are still rumored to harbor the Holy Grail (be it a stone, a riverbed, or a liquid held in a vessel), is a ruined castle, not a fort from the Year of Faith 1000. The place where the knights of spirituality gathered in the year 1000 was the monastery (with its libraries and individual cells). Many a sheep would have been seen lying down with a wolf, rapacious big cats next to lambs.

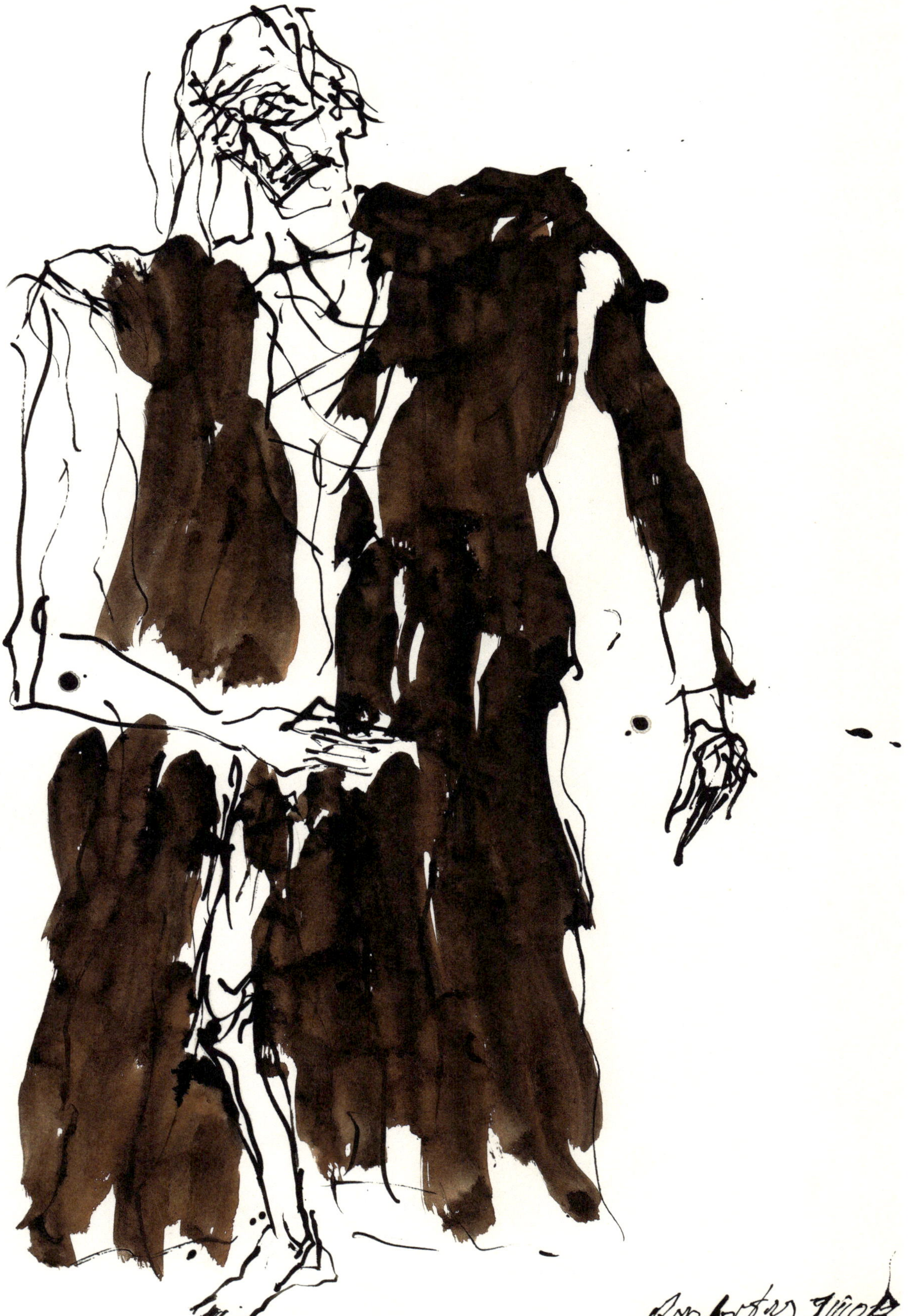

2017 Amfortas

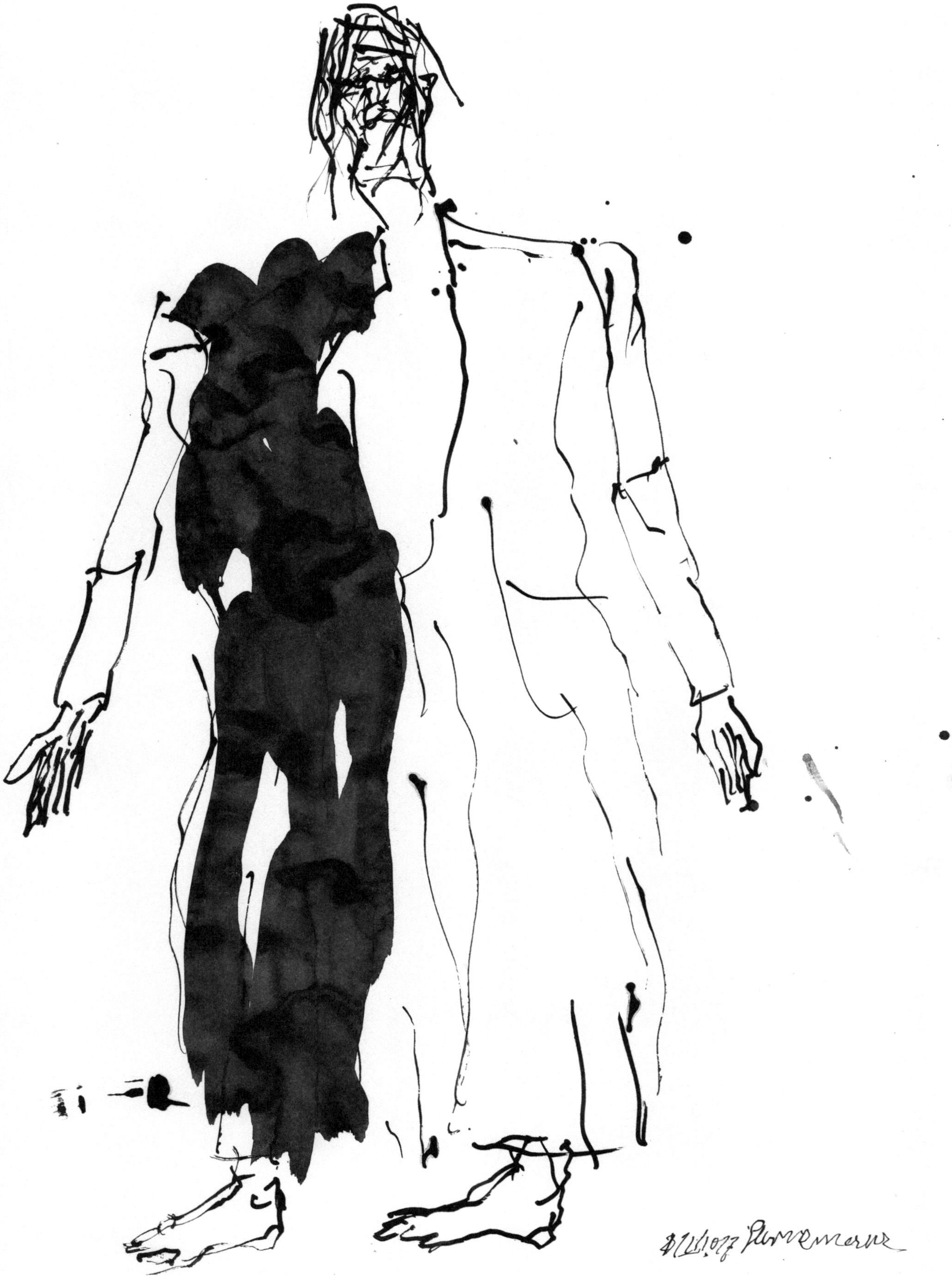

Gurnemanz 2017

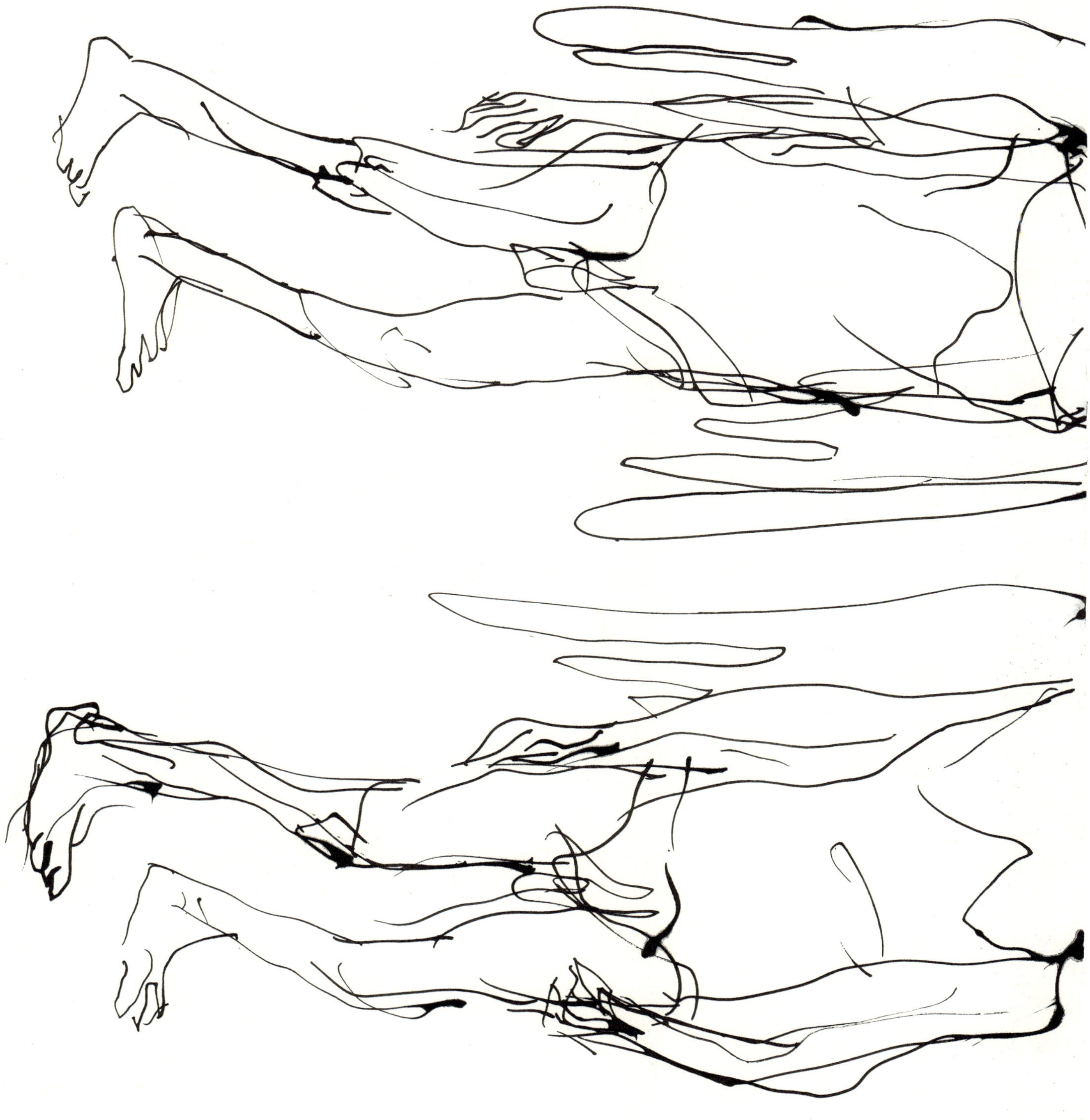

KUNDRY "LA SURZIERE," PLAYED WITH PRECISION BY A BLITHE SPIRIT WHO COULD DO THINGS QUITE DIFFERENTLY

Keeping an eye on the conductor, focused on working with the orchestra rather than on the drama's unfolding, the singers slog their way through the tough third act of *Parsifal*. Anja Kampe, the blithe spirit, is singing Kundry. In Tscherniakov's staging, Parsifal warms the feet of the laughter-prone heathen. The witch has gotten a chill in the course of her 2000-year-odyssey. Her reserves have been used up from within. In the Russian director's staging, the backstory is assumed to include a tragic love affair between Amfortas and the "Surziere." That is the reason for the ruler's wound, incurable because it's a wound of the spirit. Again and again Kundry fetches salves and healing herbs, none of which help the wound to heal over. The thing that would offer immediate succor—her total surrender, her exclusive love—is something she can't give Amfortas (can't will herself to give him, for she is besotted with Parsifal, in fact she loves him). To belong to someone like Amfortas and "heal" him—for her, that would be like perjury. Besides: the grail's all-male clique won't tolerate a relationship between a witch, and the king. But at the end of the opera her kiss really does release Amfortas from his sufferings. At that moment, Gurnemanz plunges his knife into the back of the woman who has worked the miracle—for him this is an administrative act.

While respecting the master's melodies, the admirable Anja Kampe is not prepared to cut corners or smooth over the psychology of this complicated plot. Though in real life she personally would know how to find a way out of such tortuous emotional states. Fate could be hoodwinked as effortlessly as she masters the difficult part. If she weren't in an opera, if it weren't for the director demanding it for his staging, she'd never turn her back on the orthodox Gurnemanz. Her open-hearted gaiety, her quick glance at the director is good for more than such a death.

A PARSIFAL IN THE AFRICAN SUN

In civilian life he was an icebox salesman. In 1942, outside Tobruk, he was the one who found the gap between the British pickets through which the armored wedge of the Afrikakorps could force its way into the city and all the way to the beach. All his skill at selling 1939-model iceboxes with ice-cream freezers for private homes had gone into scouting out the terrain southeast of the stronghold until he found the gap.
In the dusk of the previous day. Lent impetus by the advanced guard's aggressive élan, the 5th Armored Division had punched through the access route (only 500 meters wide) into the restricted areas. All that thanks to the intervention of the military fool whose only previous triumphs had come in icebox sales in Bielefeld. Now—in the "heat of battle," the polyphony of the moment—the THYMOS, the CRAVING FOR MORE, the speed of the forward surge and the motors should have been translated into the CHAINS AND HINGES OF PLANNING, into ENGINEERING GENIUS. Then the armored corps would have pressed on from Tobruk all the way to Port Said. There iceboxes would have been needed again, storage for vitality and for motives left to rot; however, iceboxes for feelings exist neither in fiery Africa, nor in Europe.
And not at all in the turbulent atmosphere that followed the taking of the stronghold of Tobruk. The rapture of the forward march rotted. The oil of the Orient was not seized. They would have needed a dozen such business specialists, indeed a whole regiment traveling the "Empire of the Improbable." Only in the empire of the phantasmagoric does the desert harbor miracles.

HOW I DID *NOT* BECOME A PARSIFAL

In reality, Germans' options for personal development in the 1930s were finite. In their imaginations, however, the inhabitants of Germany, including my corruptible mother, regarded it as a REAL possibility that the end of the war would bring an explosive expansion of their standard of living. And so the anxious thought of missing something made the seconds of the days seem shorter.

My mother did not regard me as a task of vital importance. And so she did not equip me with a hobby horse, fantasy sword and fool's costume. In that sense, I am no emissary. I was trained and shown the ropes in the schoolyard, not at home. I saw the distracted woman as my lodestar, but she gave me no message to take with on my way, so I have, for my own sake, invented one.

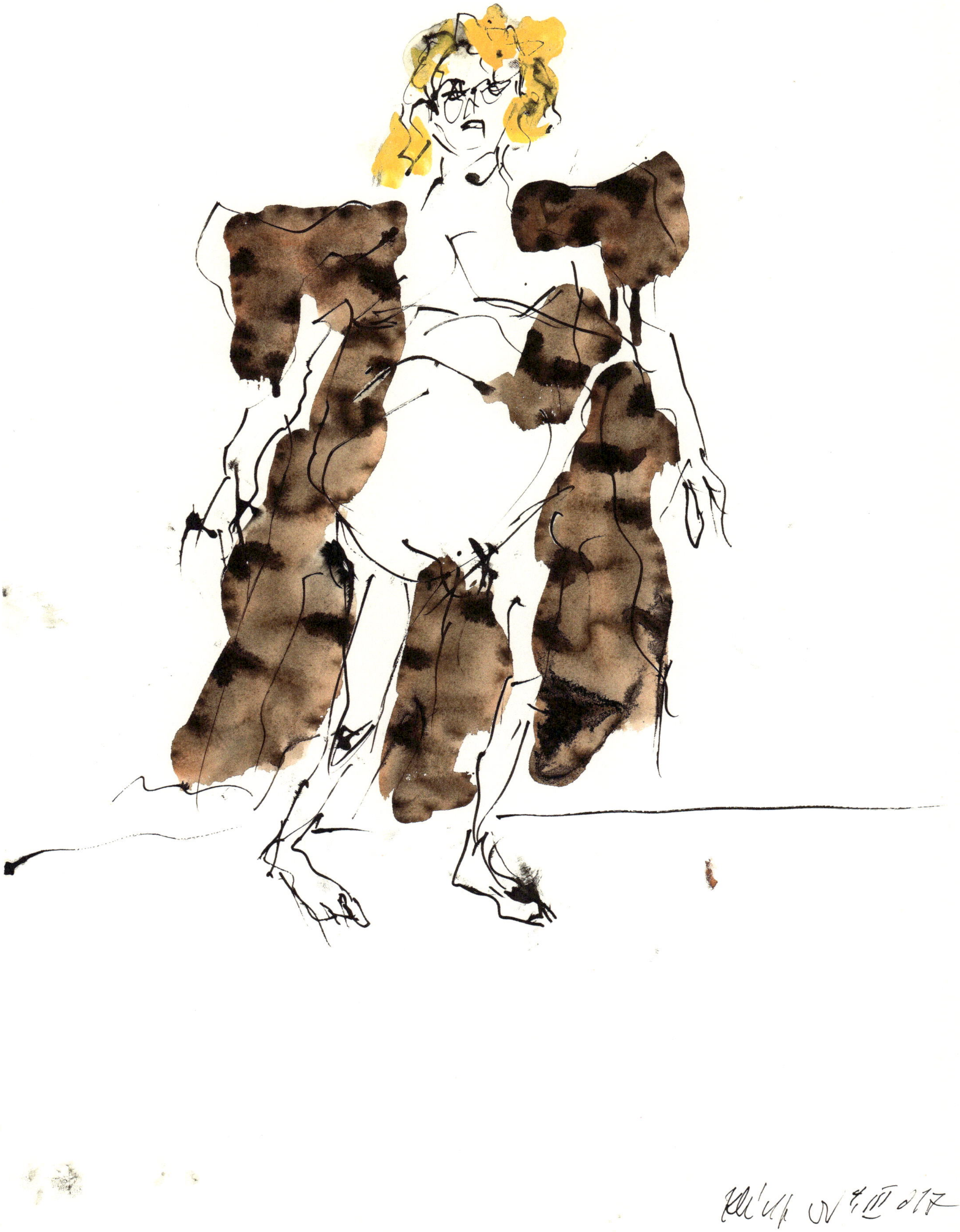

2017 Klingsor

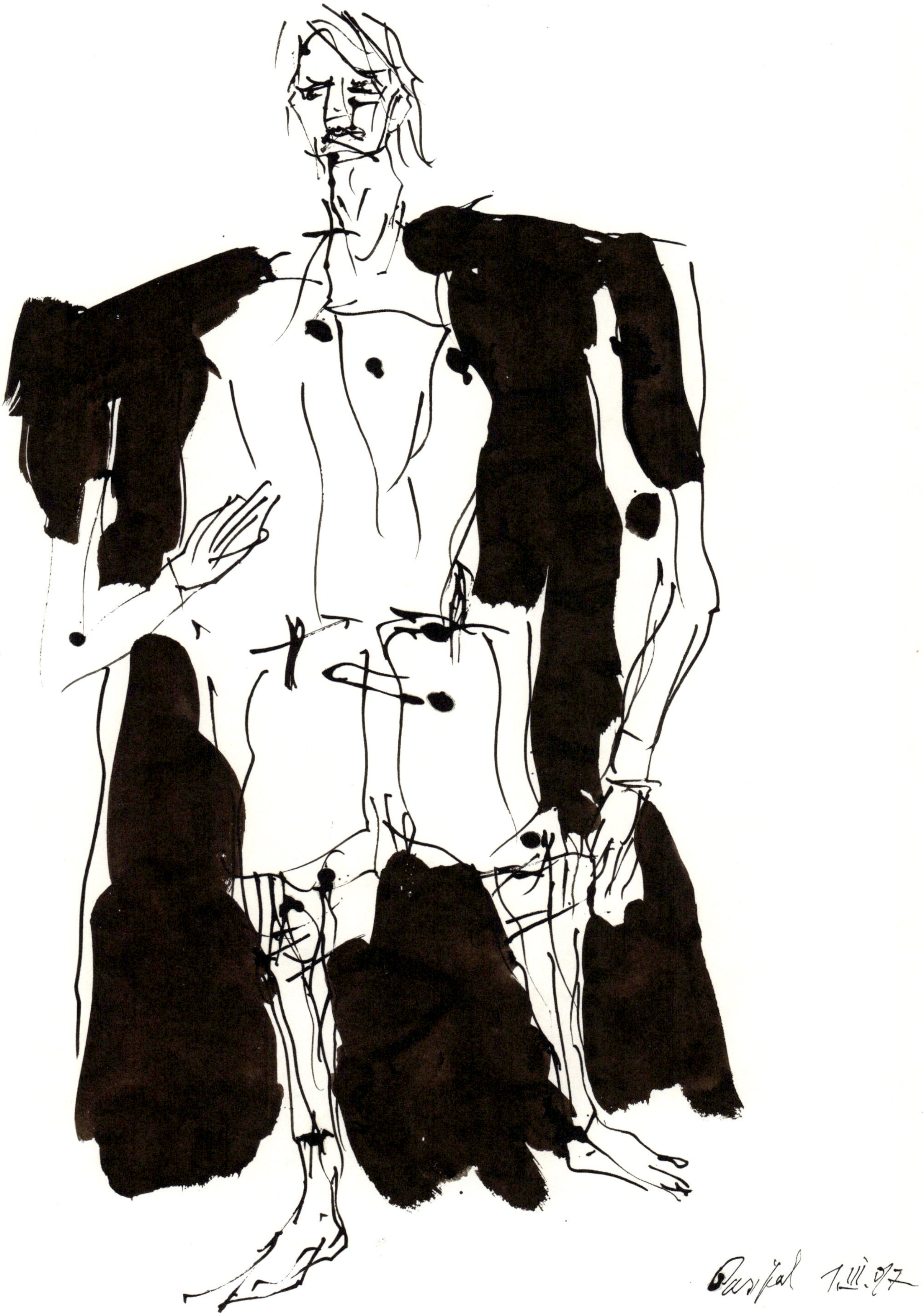
Parsifal 1.III.97

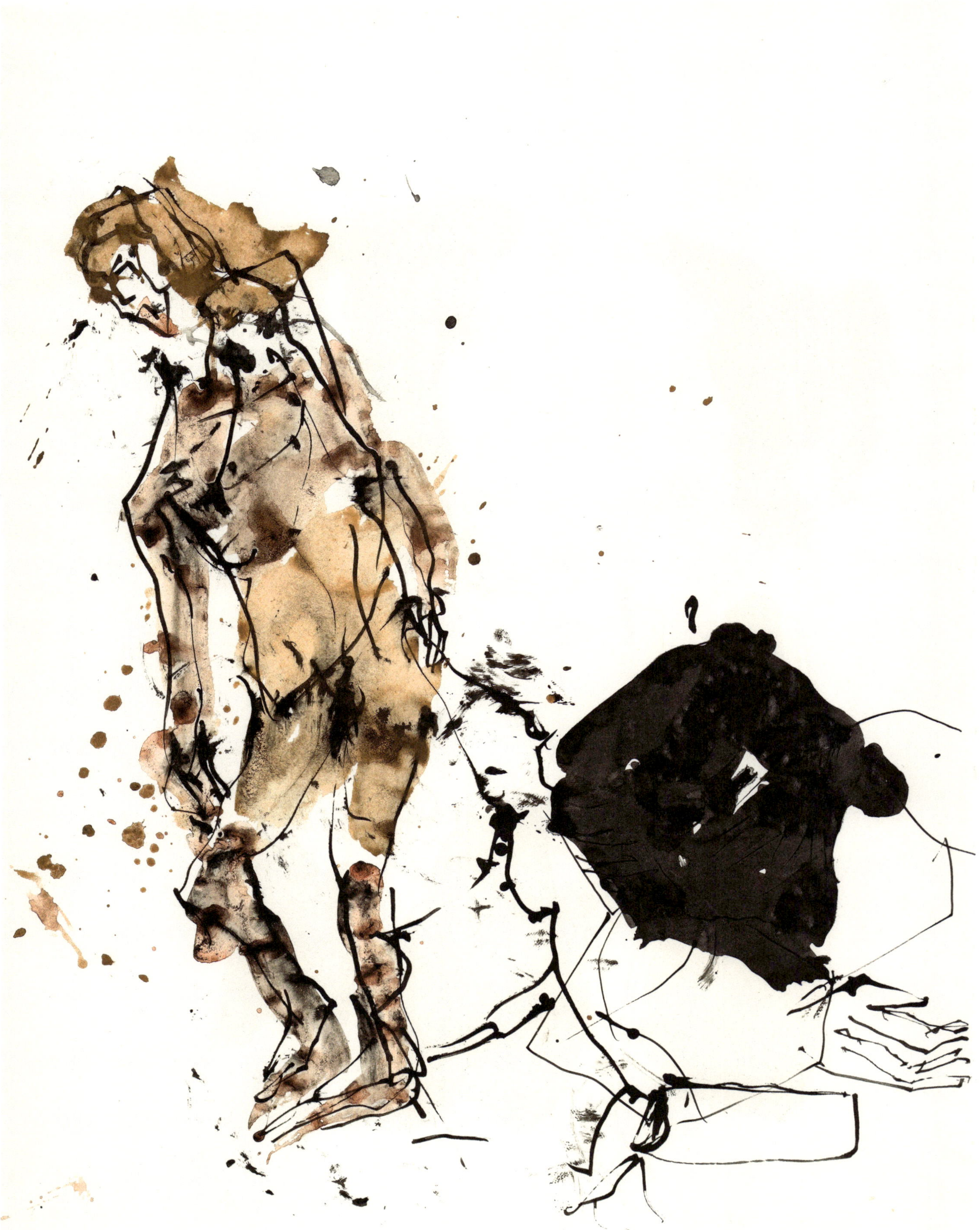

Parsifal 2017

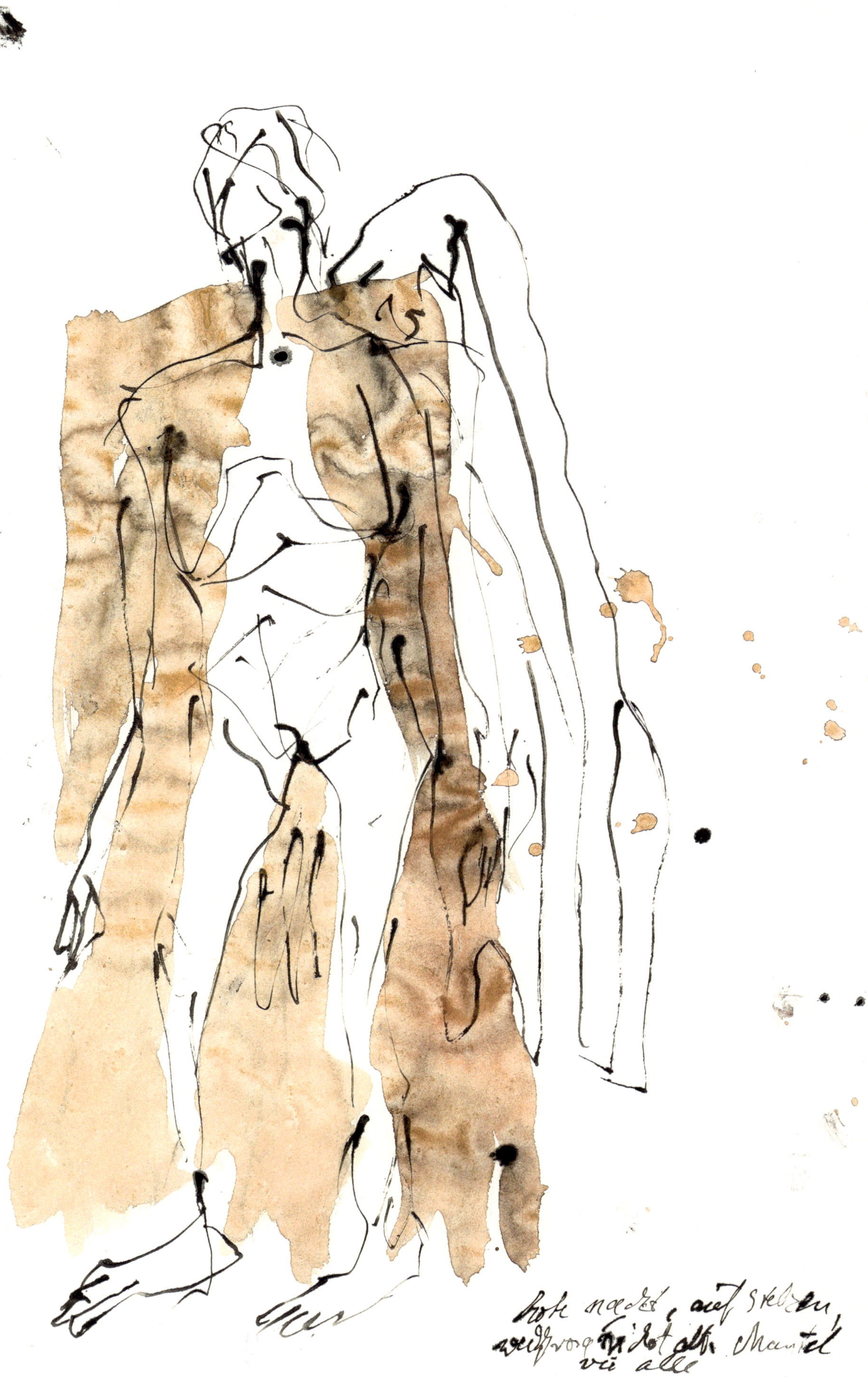

2017 Messenger

In the hours after her son's difficult birth, my sister Alexandra felt both "clairvoyant and confused." At night she talked to the "mite with the big skull" who rested replete at her side. Covered with a sheet, buttressed with pillows on both sides. "In his cot." His skull, the day before, had nearly split her birth canal.

She described to the little sleep-thing the future world that awaited him. A world not without its dangers. One day the child would assume an independent existence and leave her. That caused her pain. But for the time being he belonged to her. She was still dumbfounded. Though given a cursory wash by the hospital staff, the child was still cloaked in the microbiome of birth as though in dragon's blood. The bequest that came from her body: a protective immunity. A second skin. She, as a protective power, a grownup person, was a third skin. She wished the world were better suited for her child's safety. The outside world in 1968: protests, Vietnam, police state. She had a sense of insecurity; the words and concepts she could fall back on didn't quite fit her feelings. She knew perfectly well: no policeman was going to arrest her "little one" any time soon. But what about the minefields of history? The fangs of war? Of course, those were mere words, not the right terms for the intuition that came over her that first night. But it was a sense of the sinister. She promised the sleeper at her side that she'd stand by him all her life. And he himself would have to be forearmed. The upbringing she gave him would have to suffice. He must not become an exploiter, neither a coward nor a soldier, not a bourgeois (the term had negative associations for her), not a capitalist, but a NEW HUMAN BEING.

And that the child was. "Brand new." Yesterday and the days before that still crossways in her belly. "Breech position," the doctor on duty had said. Feet first, that was a dangerous birth position. Then, a spontaneous miracle, the child's body had turned around. Now, on top of the diapers, the sheet, the buttressing pillows, she wrapped the creature in words. The limbs were still tiny. From the neck up a "large specimen." The child had been weighed—an impressive weight.

At two in the morning, unable to sleep for excitement, she began making plans for the future. If the USA stationed missiles in the Hunsrück Mountains or the Russians stationed them in East Germany, she'd clear out to New Zealand with the baby. If her German exams and medical license weren't acknowledged there, she could still get by as a medically trained nurse. New Zealand's South Island, she knew, has a climate like Norway's. One way or the other, there the child would be far enough away from the missile installations of the two competing world powers.

AT HER NEW WORKPLACE HILDE HAD NO ONE TO TALK TO ABOUT THE GRIEF OF LOST HORIZONS

Hilde S., from Erfurt's district-level circles of the socialist aristocracy, had fled the collapse of the East German state and ended up in Switzerland. Working in a pastry shop. Moving from the icebox down the long corridor, a kind of tunnel, to the guests—for the moment uncategorizable in terms of production processes—with their coffee and torte, plum cake, cheesecake and crescent rolls. Actually, Hilde S. had wanted to retrain as an engineer. Her hero, district secretary for the Socialist Unity Party, had shot himself before the Berlin Wall fell. He'd abandoned her. The hope of progress, of one last alliance between the Party and the dissidents' Round Tables, had died out. Erased from the landscape of her expectations. There was no place but her heart to store the grief for her lost hero. She couldn't even sort through her losses. No, she was transporting cakes. Not only did she carry cakes down the long corridor or cart dishes off to the kitchen—up to four hundred times a day—she carried the hundredweight of her bitterness in her mind and on her shoulders. She had no wish for new heroes. But she couldn't relinquish her zeal—learned or innate—for reform. Grief in the wild storm of her goodwill!

If the Swiss authorities had recognized all her qualifications from the East German Workers' and Farmers' Republic, she would have adopted a child and raised it as a young socialist. The term "socialist in the 21st century" has a broad range. If she'd met a local, fallen in love and borne a child, she could have passed on a piece of her good will, forged a sword or a plowshare for progress. For now that remained "a song of the future" while she ran in rhythm down the echoing tunnel, through the seats of the café with their very different sound and then back toward the clattering world of the kitchen. "A song of the future."

ONE OF HERZELOYDE'S DOCTRINES

Herzeloyde teaches that love is not a piece of iron. Nor an iron ring, such as they put through the nose of a steer. It is not metal at all. And so it cannot be "forged." It is like spring water, but so solid that you can walk on it (and yet it is not ice). Just as mosquitos walk on the surface of a pond, light-footed in the morning sun, so does love run through the veins.

"A KNIGHT HAD FILLED RAM'S BLOOD INTO A BOTTLE"

For a moment, in the heat of the East, the hero Gahmuret, Parsifal's father, had taken off his helmet. It was made of a diamond, given him by a lady, in other words won as a favor of love. An Easterner managed to come near the hero; he'd filled ram's blood into a bottle and poured it over the helmet. Making it "soft as a sponge." Gahmuret did not suspect the weakness of his armor. The lance that struck his head that afternoon drilled through his brain and stuck out from the back of his head. Miraculously, he was able to ride away, lie down on a stretch of ground, utter a few words of confession. His retainers brought nothing home but his bloody shirt.

"AT THAT THE BLADE OF HER FORTUNE BROKE" DEATH OF THE KNIGHT OF THE IRON CROSS VON HÜNERSDORFF

On the first day of the Battle of Kursk, a piece of shrapnel shattered the arm he'd leaned on the turret of his command tank. Had the wounded man been taken to the field dressing station, he would have been saved. But with his wound hastily dressed, he insisted on smashing through two gun emplacements with his tank force. That afternoon—a shot in the head. His loyal comrades maneuvered the unconscious man, squeezed into the cabin of a Fieseler Storch (a small plane), to the field hospital in Kharkov. "The face, shot to pieces, was unrecognizable for his next of kin."

The hero's wife was the head of that field hospital. Specialists were flown in from Berlin. Every hour the commander in chief of the army group inquired into his state. After a week (and six emergency operations), the dream of his troops, Major General von Hünersdorff, was dead. All seven skins protecting the man proved illusory. The skin—with traces of a sunburn from early July still on his shoulders, rubbed with cod liver oil—that's the way of things; skin is not invulnerable under fire. A second skin was the fortunes of war, the jaunty cap on his head, the aura of a man "whom no bullet can strike." That was no skin in the strict sense, it was a special form of courage: the quickness with which tanks could change position. His tank always confounded the foe's expectations. The third skin was the vigilance of his comrades, who loved their idol, blasted many dangers out of his way: shared courage, a cloud of motives. At four a.m., when they revved up their motors, that cocoon was still intact.

Then, as the fourth skin, the newfangled tanks with metal reinforced by concrete slabs, the integrated retardation of enemy missiles. But the rampart of built-in invention deceived the occupants insofar as the Russian artillery had equally novel high-speed ammunition that no one had known about before that morning. It sliced open the steel of the tank's skin as though it were "made of sponge."

The innermost (fifth) skin that protected him when all the other skins failed was his confidence. It consisted—as with jellyfish—of a body without a head: sheer network. That sort of confidence is distinct from self-assurance. The weeks in which the army command had postponed the attack, the sweltering heat by day, the thunderstorms at night—in other words the whole waiting game—had worn down that confidence.

A further tough skin (the sixth), like the calloused skin of Siegfried, was the reputation that preceded Hünersdorff's tank force and had often confused the enemy's senses like a CLOAK OF INVISIBILITY: the horror, the anticipation of what would come with iron brutality as soon as the tanks loomed over the hill. That was gone for good in the Battle of Kursk, the fighters on both sides had not realized it yet that first day. The last skin (the seventh) in which von Hünersdorff might have sought refuge was the art of military medicine. One year later (they learned quickly in that war) they could have successfully scraped together a destroyed brain like the shrapnel-pierced one of the Major General and kept it at least fractionally functional. Like an ANGEL OF THAT SEVENTH SKIN, the young Frau von Hünersdorff stood at the head of the doomed man.

And so a hero such as that man had seven protective skins, all of which failed: first, the one around his heart; second, the one around his body; the skin of his troop; the iron skin of his tank; the quick reaction (the antithesis of armor, opening itself to danger and escaping it through defiance); sixth, action at a distance; seventh, conduir amour (never had the head of the field hospital urged on the doctors as in the hour before the death of her beloved).

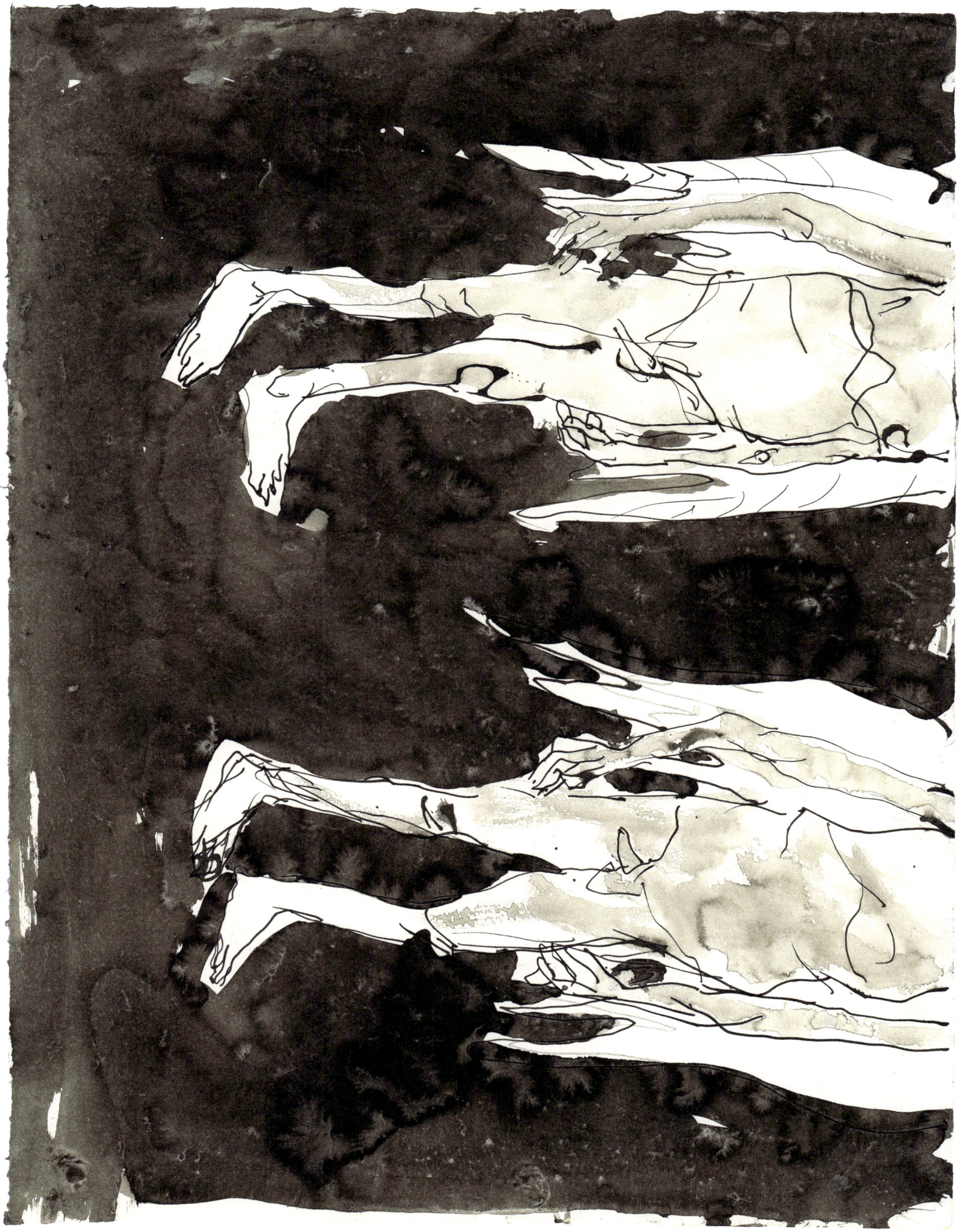

2016 Untitled

“The face,
shot
to pieces,

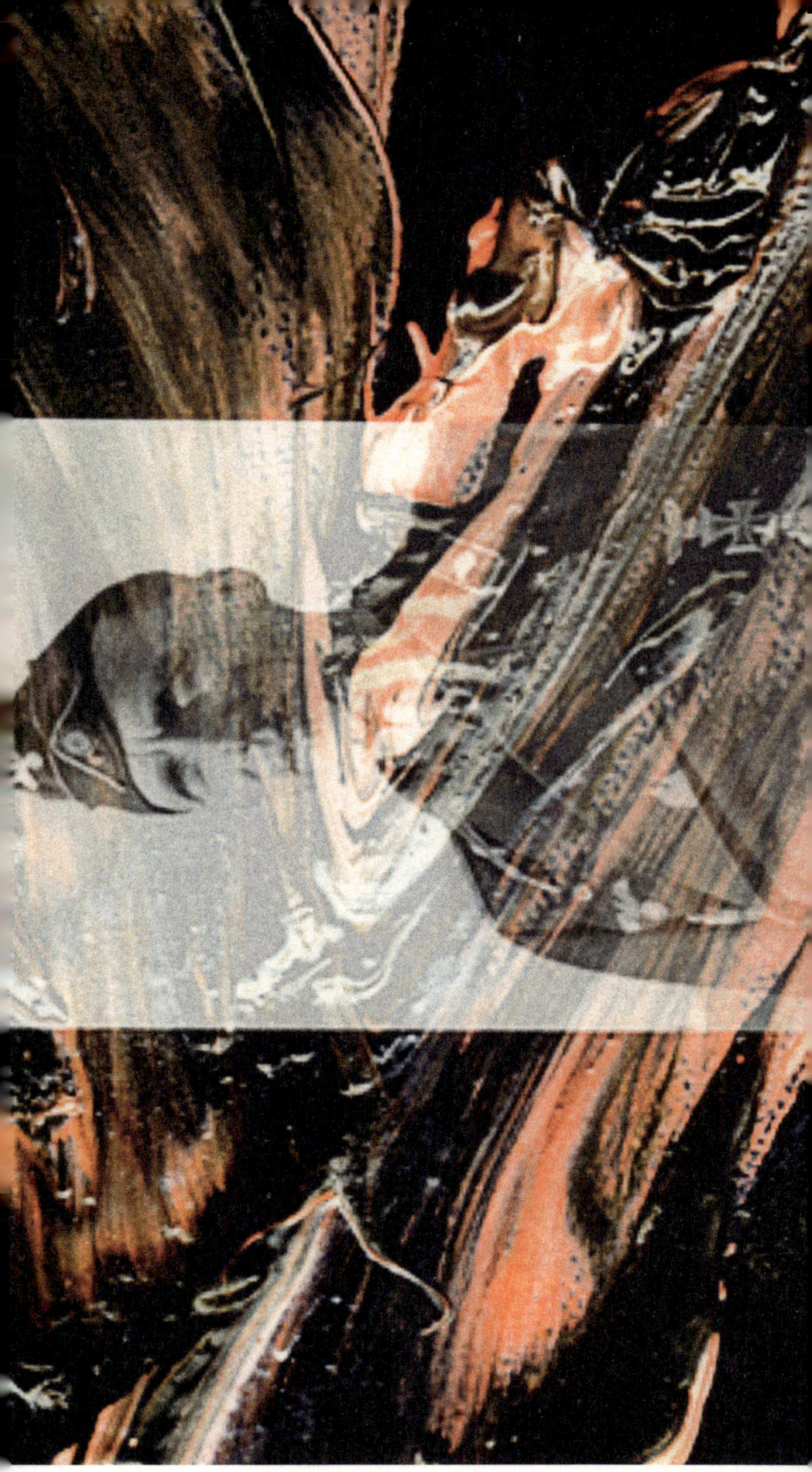

Film still from *Hommage für Georg Baselitz*, 2018

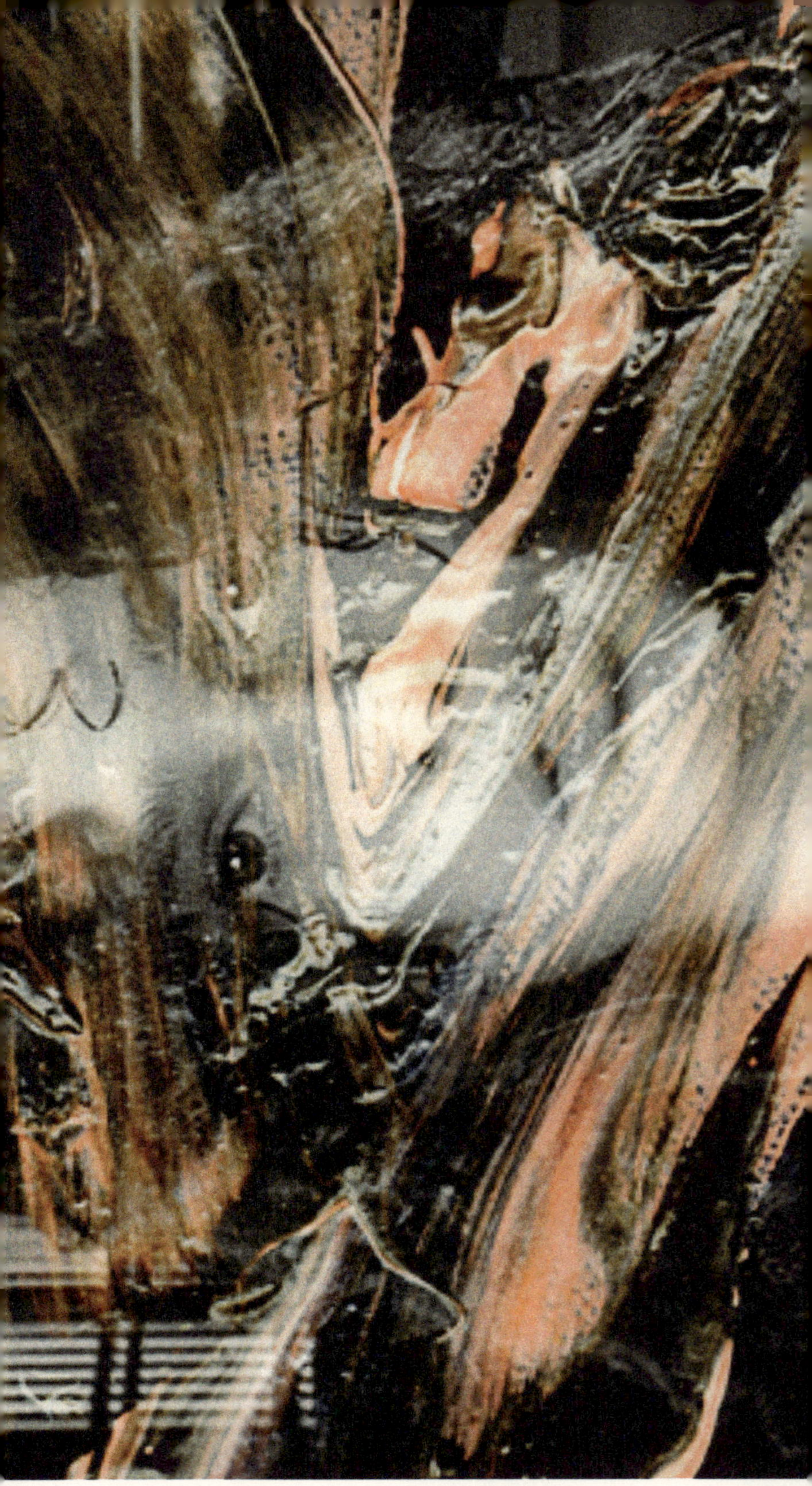

Film still from *Hommage für Georg Baselitz*, 2018

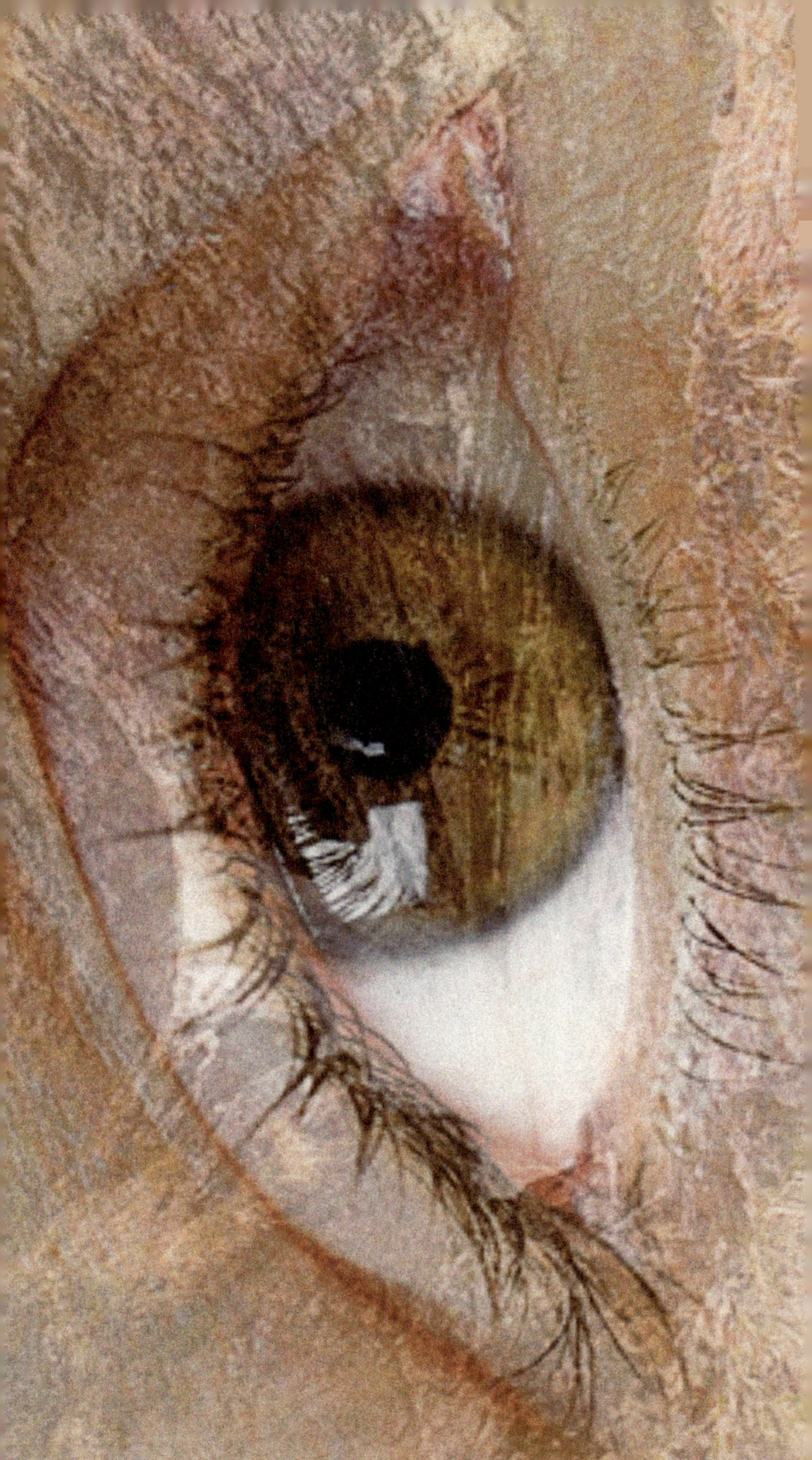

Poster for Baselitz' exhibition at the Fondation Beyeler in Basel, 2018

was
unrecognizable for
his next of kin”

“At that
the blade of her
fortune broke”

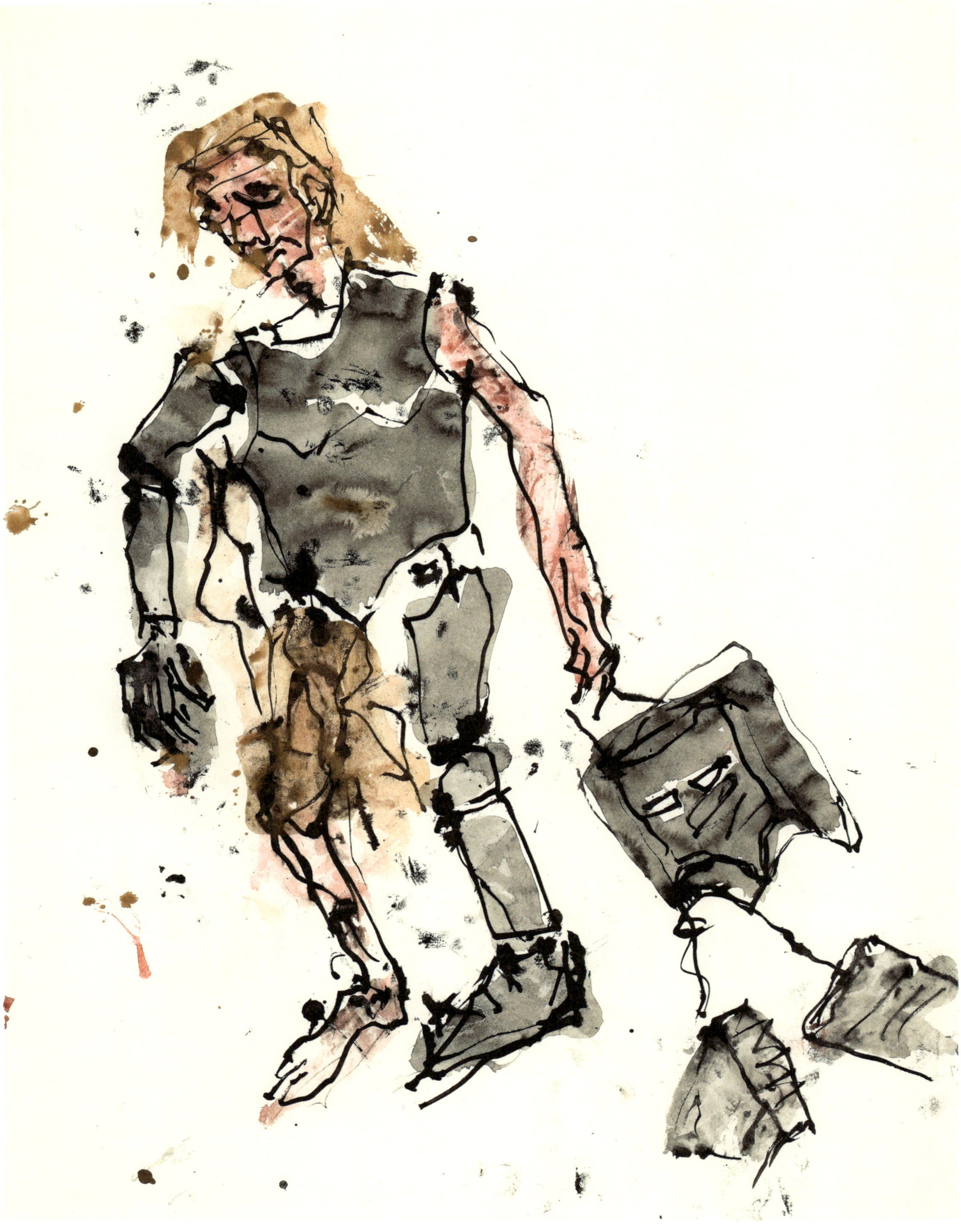

Parsifal 2017

THE EMERGENCE OF SALVATION FROM "CONTAMINATION" / COUNTER TO ALL THEORIES OF PURITY

Our cosmos has been producing nuclear waste for over thirteen billion years. At first (as soon as they take form) the suns consist of blue and white light. A pure mixture of hydrogen and helium. But each time one of those radiant stars collapses, an explosion ensues, ejecting a gush of incubated matter from its interior and transforming it into dust. When nucleosynthesis has produced enough heavy elements—nitrogen, neon, silicon, iron—in nature's atomic furnaces, this "contamination" gives rise to the rebirth of the suns and, in our cells, to the tiny nuclei that can decide between life and death. In this sense, the fool's narrative of Parsifal, the grail seeker, is about "an impure idiot."

HOW MUCH OF A FOOL DOES SOMEONE NEED TO BE TO TRIUMPH AS OFTEN AS PARSIFAL AND AGAINST SUCH STRONG OPONNENTS?

The hero's arms, legs, shoulders, neck—for Baselitz, all these are autonomous creatures. Things are autonomous creatures as well. The hero Parsifal tugs his armor along behind him like a toy cannon.
A real person might have the shoulders of his father Gahmuret, the wrists and palms of his mother Herzeloyde, his thighs perhaps from a future lover's dream world, his ideas from a god or from his as-yet-unborn sons. DNA works in both directions: from the future into the pasts and from the pasts into the present. The collection of disparate traits that makes up a person, a hero or an anti-hero, is always good for a battle, for an error, and for the general quest for happiness. Indeed, one could say that only the confrontation with fate unites a person's separately marching characters. In quiet times the limbs come asunder. There is no such thing as heroism from pure insight.

LAUGHTER FROM THE DEPTHS OF THE ORCHESTRA

The music lover Joachim Kaiser was lounging in an armchair. Reclining rather than sitting. I don't believe—he opened the debate—that in his musical heart of hearts, which never deceived him, Wagner had a pronounced sense of Christianity. Thus, Kaiser reasoned, he will have seen nothing shocking in the claim that the heroine Kundry laughed at the sight of Christ bearing the cross. The crown of thorns was perched grotesquely on his head. That sort of laughter is spontaneously triggered by the diaphragm. It does not express the consciousness or the character or any specific culpability. Rather, the urge to laugh arises irresistibly, and more swiftly than any other affect. Why shouldn't Kundry be allowed to laugh?

And during the *Bühnenweihfestspiel* listeners don't actually hear Kundry laugh in any of the three acts. Only once do they hear laughter, in the depths of the orchestra. Not a leitmotif, merely a short sequence of notes. It could also be a sob. Or a cheer.

Besides, Joachim Kaiser went on, the proper theological interpretation—that is, not just Wagner's private opinion—regards jubilation as a correct response to the crucifixion, for after all it redeems the world. Ernst Jünger—Kaiser emphasized this—pointed out Mary Magdalene's jubilation when facing the cross. In that instant she was unable to distinguish her suffering, her pain over the torments of the beloved, from the bright lightning flash of knowledge: the prophecy of the Last Judgement.

Why, then—Kaiser puts the question more sharply—is Kundry forced to spend two thousand years "contaminating" heroes, tempting them against her will, as though suffering from a compulsion? What is more, doing this as the slave of a faithless, malicious sorcerer—merely because she couldn't help laughing at a certain moment? In this tranquil conversational atmosphere—night had fallen, drinks were provided, Kaiser did most of the talking himself—this self-declared Wagner fan voiced his impression that subcutaneously, that is, under the skin of the story, a "second plot" was unfolding, understandable only through the spirit of the music. And the music had nothing at all to do with some obscure fit of laughter. It is almost always worthwhile to get to the bottom of these sorts of riddles. These sorts of "concealed texts," virtual palimpsests ("overprinting," "overwriting"), give rise to arrhythmias such as in the song "Die Fahne hoch." In the verse "Comrades who Red Front and reactionaries have shot, march in spirit in our ranks ...", the word order and emphasis leaves it unclear who killed whom. The riddle is solved when you learn that the song's tune, and thus its rhythm, meaning and emphasis, originates in an older song from the colonial period, sung from the heart by homesick colonists in German East Africa. In that colonial song, the emphasis made sense. In Horst Wessel's subsequent adaptation to a completely different text, the sense of the emphasis has gotten lost. In the colonial song, a homicidal robber unwittingly meets up with his brother. About to plunge in the knife, he recognizes his brother from a mark on his chest. The two men embrace each other, rather than one of them getting killed. That was not the sense and content of the Horst Wessel song.

Similarly, he, Kaiser, conjectured that Kundry's foolish fixation that forced her to seduce men and plunge them into ruin might have quite a different cause than her supposed laughter at the suffering of a god. Jochen Kaiser had talked himself into a frenzy. He loved Wagner's music, and as he spoke, he heard it inside him. And so he ramped up his thoughts: he had his doubts, he said, that Kundry was even a woman at all. Similarly, it was uncertain to what extent Parsifal was a mere man. As the "very pattern" of his beautiful, strong mother, at least half of him came from Eve's rib, perhaps only some small part from the rib of his father.

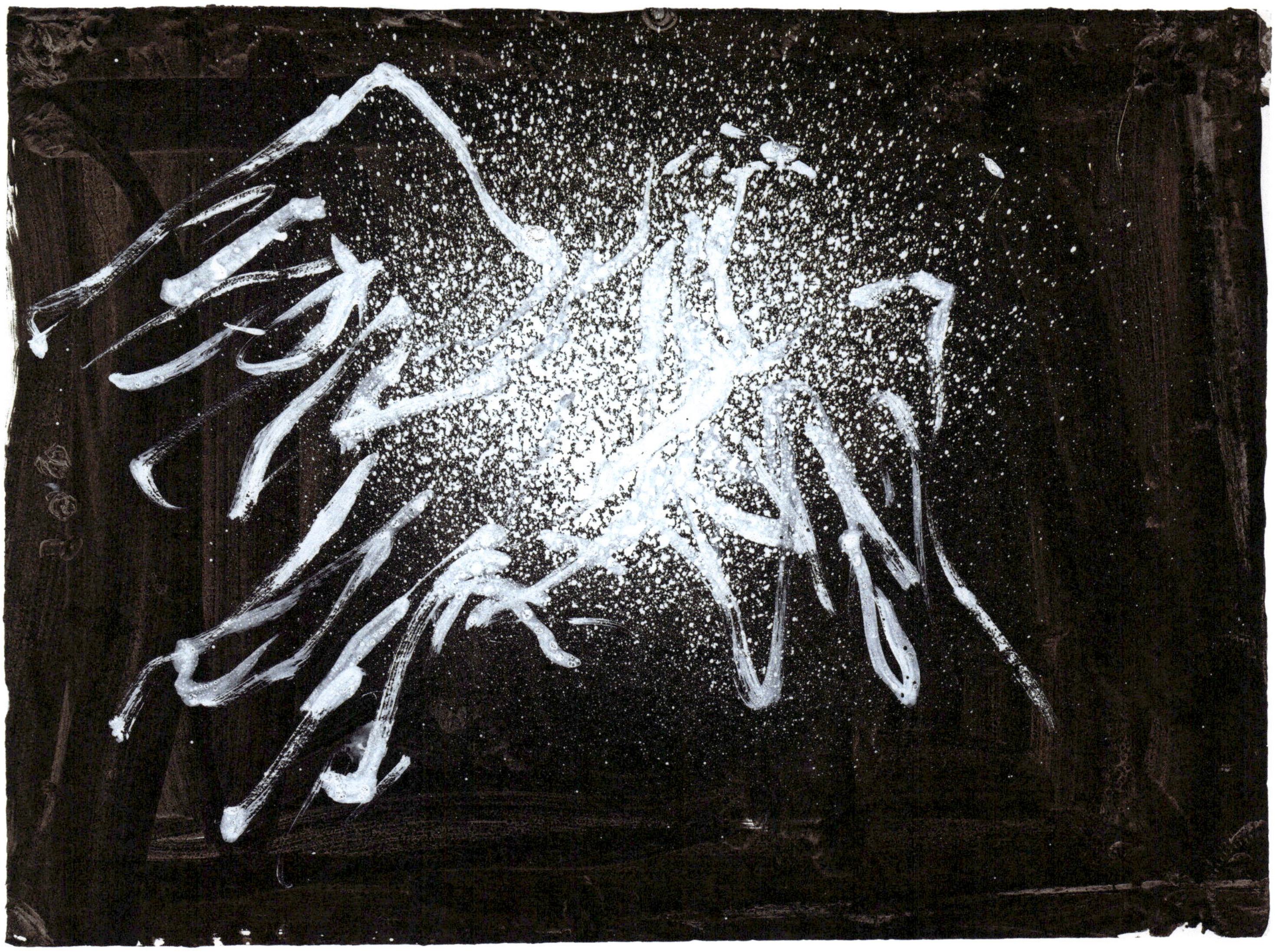

2018

Backdrop dove

PARSIFAL CONTAINER
Georg Baselitz
Alexander Kluge

TEXT
Alexander Kluge

ILLUSTRATIONS
Georg Baselitz

GRAPHIC DESIGN
Fabian Bremer, Pascal Storz

TYPESETTING
Hannes Drißner

TRANSLATION INTO ENGLISH
Isabel Cole

PROOFREADING
Jan Caspers

IMAGE PROCESSING, PRINTING AND BINDING
DZA Druckerei zu Altenburg GmbH

PUBLISHED BY
Spector Books
Harkortstraße 10
04107 Leipzig
www.spectorbooks.com

DISTRIBUTION

Germany, Austria:
GVA, Gemeinsame Verlagsauslieferung
Göttingen GmbH & Co. KG
www.gva-verlage.de

Switzerland:
AVA Verlagsauslieferung AG
www.ava.ch

France, Belgium:
Interart Paris
www.interart.fr

UK:
Central Books Ltd
www.centralbooks.com

USA, Canada, Central and South America, Africa:
ARTBOOK / D.A.P.
www.artbook.com

South Korea:
The Book Society
www.thebooksociety.org

Japan:
twelvebooks
www.twelve-books.com

Australia, New Zealand:
Perimeter Distribution
www.perimeterdistribution.com

First edition: 2020
Printed in Germany

ISBN 978-3-95905-382-2